I0811662

Antique Majolica Around the House

Jeffrey B. Snyder

Schiffer Publishing Ltd

4880 Lower Valley Road, Atglen, PA 19310 USA

Dedication

To Sherry—for the twenty years of love and laughter we have shared, and for all the years yet to come!

Library of Congress Cataloging-in-Publication Data

Snyder, Jeffrey B.
Antique majolica : around the house / by Jeffrey B. Snyder.
p. cm.
ISBN 0-7643-2134-X (hardcover)
1. Majolica, Victorian—Collectors and collecting—Catalogs. I. Title.

NK4315.S58 2004
738.3'72'075—dc22

2004015490

Designed by "Ellen J. Taltoan"
Type set in Zapf Chancery Bd BT/Souvenir Lt BT

ISBN: 0-7643-2134-X
Printed in China

Published by Schiffer Publishing Ltd.
4880 Lower Valley Road
Atglen, PA 19310
Phone: (610) 593-1777; Fax: (610) 593-2002
E-mail: Info@schifferbooks.com

Contents

Acknowledgments 4
Introduction 5
Majolica's Many Forms 7
Majolica's Manufacturers 19
In Britain 20
On the Continent 28
In the United States 37
Majolica's Manufacturers' Marks 43
Dating Majolica with Manufacturers' Marks 44
Registration Marks 46
Majolica's Values 47
Friendly Advice 50
Majolica Around the House 53
House Styles 53
Entering the House 54
Private Spaces 59
Bedroom 59
Boudoir/library/study 63
Breakfast room/sitting room 65
Kitchen 77
Nursery/children's bedrooms 105
Public Places 107
Billiard-/Smoking-room 107
Conservatory/porch/garden 115
Dining room 130
Drawing room/parlor 206
Entryway 231
Last Words – Majolica's Significance 234
Bibliography 237
Index 239

Acknowledgments

I would like to thank the people who made this project a success. If it were not so repetitive, most of the photo captions in this book would end *Courtesy of Majolica Auctions, M. Strawser.* Michael G. Strawser, owner of Majolica Auctions, was instrumental to this project, and to several others that have gone before. Mr. Strawser allowed us access to the March 26-27, 2004, auction site in Hatfield, Pennsylvania, prior to the auction. There we photographed the vast majority of the beautiful majolica antiques appearing in this book. Among them are majolica items from the collection of actress Lauren Bacall. If you would like to contact Mr. Strawser about upcoming auctions, he may be reached through the following address: 200 North Main, P.O. Box 332, Wolcottville, Indiana 46795 or through his web site: www.majolicaauctions.com.

I also extend warm thanks to Skinner, Inc. Boston, for allowing me access to images of their impressive majolica antiques. Their help was also greatly appreciated.

I also wish to thank Donna Baker, Mark Bowyer, and Melissa Cordona, who spent a long night with me photographing majolica. Their efforts were essential in the creation of this beautiful book.

Finally, I would like to thank everyone else who helped make this book a reality. You are a truly talented bunch and you know who you are! Thank you, everyone.

Introduction

From the 1850s through the early twentieth century, majolica wares were produced in such a wide variety of forms, from the thoroughly useful to the outrageously ornamental, they could literally be put to use in every room of a Victorian home. Majolica umbrella stands stood ready in the entryway; platters and oyster plates graced the dining room table; whimsical pitchers brightened cook's day in the kitchen; bright tea sets served a family's afternoon tea in the sitting room; majolica figurines in human, mythological, and animal forms cavorted in whatnot cabinets in the parlor; spill vases resided on the mantles; desk sets shone brightly in the library or the boudoir; dressing and chamber sets were at home in the bedrooms; miniature tea sets, fanciful figurines, and amusing banks found use in the children's rooms and nursery; and formidable pedestaled jardinières vied with the ornamental plants they held for the viewer's attention in the conservatory … or anywhere else the soothing, green touch of nature was deemed appropriate.

Victorian gentlemen and ladies were required by the rules of etiquette to leave their umbrellas and walking sticks in the entryway when coming to call. Cobalt water lily and bamboo umbrella stand, manufactured by Joseph Holdcroft (Longton, Staffordshire, England, 1865-1939), 23" h. This umbrella stand is valued around $4,400+; however, it sold in 2004 at auction for $3,250.

These majolica figures would grace any Victorian drawing room. **Left:** a rare figure of lady gathering wheat in field, by Wedgwood (Josiah Wedgwood (& Sons Ltd.) Staffordshire, England, c. 1759-present), 20.5" h. **Right:** a rare Wedgwood figure of lady with a jug of water at the spring, 21" h. These figures sold in 2004 at auction for $2,500 each.

Entering the conservatory, it would be difficult to miss this monumental floor jardinière with large vine handles and rim of grape clusters by W. T. Copeland (& Sons Ltd.) (Stoke, Staffordshire, England, 1847-present). Cobalt ground with faces of mythological figures in high relief, 29" w., 17" h. This massive jardinière sold in 2004 at auction for $3,350.

Majolica's Many Forms

Majolica was soft-bodied earthenware molded in low or high relief decoration and glazed with a broad palette of brilliant lead glaze colors. Majolica was at its height of popularity from the 1850s through the mid-1880s. By the late 1880s, majolica was overproduced and quality was on the decline. Majolica wares would continue to be produced on into the twentieth century, mainly in Continental Europe and Australia, but the majolica appearing on the American market by that time was largely comprised of inexpensive premium items and carnival prizes.

Mermaids and shell table center with laurel garlands, by Minton (Stoke, Staffordshire, England, 1793-present), the base impressed with the date code for 1866, 17.5" l., 10" h. This impressive table centerpiece brought over $9,700 at auction in 2004.

The English potter Herbert Minton, working with the French ceramicist Jean François Léon Arnoux (Minton's art director from 1849 to 1892), created Victorian majolica in 1849 and introduced it to the public in grand fashion at the Crystal Palace Exhibition in London in 1851, the first world's fair. In name and form, Minton's early majolica emulated Renaissance maiolica wares, fifteenth century artifacts much coveted by Victorian antiquarians. The original maiolica is well described in the trade journal *Manufacturer and Builder* as follows:

> The name majolica [throughout history writers have referred to this Renaissance era tin-glazed ware as either maiolica or majolica] refers to a certain style of painting on terra-cotta or earthenware, which appears to have originated in the island of Majorca, which the ancient Tuscan writers called Maiolica. From this island its use is supposed to have been introduced into Italy, where it was first practiced by Lucca della Robbia, who is the reputed discoverer of the white stanniferous (tin compound) enamel with which he covered the terra-cotta. At his time (he was born in 1400) only crude pottery was used in Italy, as well as over the civilized world at that period, and it was only towards the end of the fifteenth century that furnaces and workshops were erected in Tuscany, the Romagnes, etc., where the pieces of majolica were manufactured which now, on account of their beauty and historical interest, are the admiration of collectors of antiquities. The oldest piece of this kind in existence bears the date 1438, and was made by Lucca della Robbia; but several other pieces made in various Italian cities, were made in 1477 and 1482. (1876, 257)

The British pottery firm Wedgwood joined in majolica production in the 1860s with great success. A salmon platter with a rare yellow background color, by Wedgwood, measuring 25" l. x 12.75" w. This rarity of this platter with the yellow ground color is reflected in the price of $13,750 it brought at auction in 2004.

For Victorians who strove to emulate the scholarly antiquarians but did not have sufficient means, Minton's majolica would provide a suitable air of antiquity once ensconced on the mantle. The Wedgwood pottery company, established by Josiah Wedgwood in the mid-eighteenth century, entered the majolica market in the 1860s. Josiah Wedgwood had been fascinated with antiquities himself. In 1841, it was reported that Josiah Wedgwood's home in Shelton, England, was decorated with reproductions of ancient Etruscan vases. The Wedgwood manufactory's early majolica was similar to Minton's. Not only did both firms' management appreciate antiquities, but Wedgwood also hired a number of Minton's better known designers on a freelance basis to develop the firm's majolica lines. By the 1880s, Wedgwood would carry over 350 different majolica designs.

While some early examples from the 1850s and 1860s were spectacular and expensive works of art, the vast majority of majolica wares were more affordable. In form and decoration, majolica wares reflected the many, shifting passions of the Victorian age. A potent combination of Victorian romanticism and naturalism provided the impetus for capturing much of the natural world in majolica ceramics. Charles Darwin's *On the Origin of Species by Means of Natural Selection,* published in 1859, also fueled the fascination with the natural world.

A potent combination of Victorian romanticism and naturalism provided the impetus for capturing much of the natural world in majolica. Double strawberry server with squirrel handle, turquoise ground, George Jones (& Sons, Ltd.) (Staffordshire, England, 1861-1907), great color and detail, 13.5" l. $2,035-2,240.

Oak leaf tray with birds on branch at each end with acorns, each bird's head is a lid which lifts off to create an inkwell or preserve pots, Minton, shape no. 1458, date code for 1870, 13" l. $3,500+.

Jumbo

During his four year tour of North America with the Barnum and Bailey Circus, Jumbo the elephant was a colossal hit with the public. Souvenirs of all sorts were created featuring Jumbo's image, including this Jumbo elephant majolica pitcher, unmarked, 6.5" h. $250-300.

Jumbo the elephant was captured on the plains of Abyssinia in 1861. After several stops, he found a home briefly at the London Zoo. There his trainer, Matthew "Scotty" Scott, taught Jumbo to accept a multi-seat "howdah" on his back and take marveling visitors for rides. Part of Jumbo's mighty size may be attributed to the peanuts and English buns given him by his admirers.

Phineas T. Barnum, showman and purveyor of "unique" entertainment who had once displayed the upper half of a monkey's skeleton attached to the lower half of a fish as the "Fejee mermaid" and billed Joice Heth, an elderly African-American woman, as George Washington's 161-year-old nanny, purchased Jumbo from the London Zoo in 1882 to become a star attraction in the newly established Barnum and Bailey Circus. Britons, including Queen Victoria herself, were enraged by the sale. However, on April 9, 1882, Jumbo arrived at the Manhattan Battery pier. With typical Barnum fanfare, the elephant was paraded down Broadway in a wagon hauled by sixteen horses, several hundred strong men, and a battery of circus elephants. Thus began Jumbo's showbiz career.

Jumbo toured North America for four years as part of the Barnum and Bailey Circus. To enhance the impression of great size, Jumbo was featured with a baby elephant. Gingerbread replaced English buns as Jumbo's favorite treat from fans. It was estimated that sixteen million adults and four million children paid to see the elephant billed as "The Towering Monarch of His Mighty Race." In the United States, and back in England, Jumbo products were sold to an adoring public, including: majolica, cigars, canes, hats, bracelets, earrings, fans, trading cards, and anything else that could have the famous elephant's image applied to it. (Wilson 2002)

Thrush bird on leaf and floral tray with rare pink ground, George Jones, c. 1874, 10" w. In the turquoise ground glaze color, this tray is valued around $1,850-2,035; however, in the rare pink ground glaze color, it sold for $2,500 at auction in 2004.

English-trained Australian potters found majolica a suitable medium for depicting Australia's native flora and fauna. In Australia, the passion for majolica developed out of an 1850s gold rush and a subsequent demand for decorative ceramics among the newly moneyed classes. Majolica would be produced in Australia from the 1860s to the 1940s. Many denizens of the outback were immortalized in majolica over those long decades.

Bird on oak leaf tray, Minton, shape no. 1331, 8". $1,420-1,565.

Cobalt bird and pond lily serving tray, Wedgwood, 9.75" w. $2,000+.

Charles Darwin's *On the Origins of Species by Means of Natural Selection* also fueled the fascination with the natural world. Monkey and coconut figural teapot, Minton, 8.5" l., 6" h. While the value of this teapot has been estimated around $4,600-5,100, in 2004, this teapot sold at auction for $5,750.

As the nineteenth century progressed, many passing artistic styles were captured in bright majolica glazes and imaginative majolica forms. Japanese design sensibilities and decorative motifs were expressed in majolica wares following several world's fairs of the 1860s where Japanese wares created a real stir, including the South Kensington Exhibition of 1862 and the Paris Exhibition of 1867.

After Japanese designs caused a stir at two world's fairs of the 1860s, Japanese decorative motifs were added to the range of styles decorating majolica. Diamond-shaped cachepot, George Jones, cobalt ground with bamboo borders, storks, water lilies and flowers in relief, outstanding color and detail, 11.5" l., 7" h. In 2004, this cachepot sold for $6,325 at auction.

Opposite page:
Sunflower oyster plate with lavender rim, Samuel Lear (Hanley, Staffordshire, England, 1876-1886), 9.75" d. $3,240-3,600.

Later majolica forms of the last quarter of the nineteenth and early twentieth centuries reflected other stylistic trends as well. The Arts and Crafts Movement was a reaction to industrialization. As the Industrial Revolution swept through Western society during the Victorian era, families attracted by new job opportunities moved from rural to urban communities, radically changing their daily lives and routines. Husbands and wives who had once worked side by side on the land were separated, he going off to work in the factory or office and she left to tend to the home or to take up job opportunities that were slowly opening to women. Families were distanced from the land. Many living in crowded, dirty cities and working in poor conditions for low wages looked back wistfully to an earlier, simpler, agrarian age.

The Arts and Crafts movement originated in England and spread to the United States, inspired by the teachings and examples of William Morris and John Ruskin. The ideal of the movement was to allow individual artists to create wares in the decorative arts that were beautifully handcrafted products from nature. Such products were to be both useful items and works of art. The decorative motifs taken from nature reflect that desire for closeness with the natural world that was largely lost in the urban setting. It was also hoped that the presence of art would elevate social values. The Arts and Crafts Movement would remain influential in the United States into the first quarter of the twentieth century.

French Art Nouveau two handled floral vases, 13" h. $500-550 each.

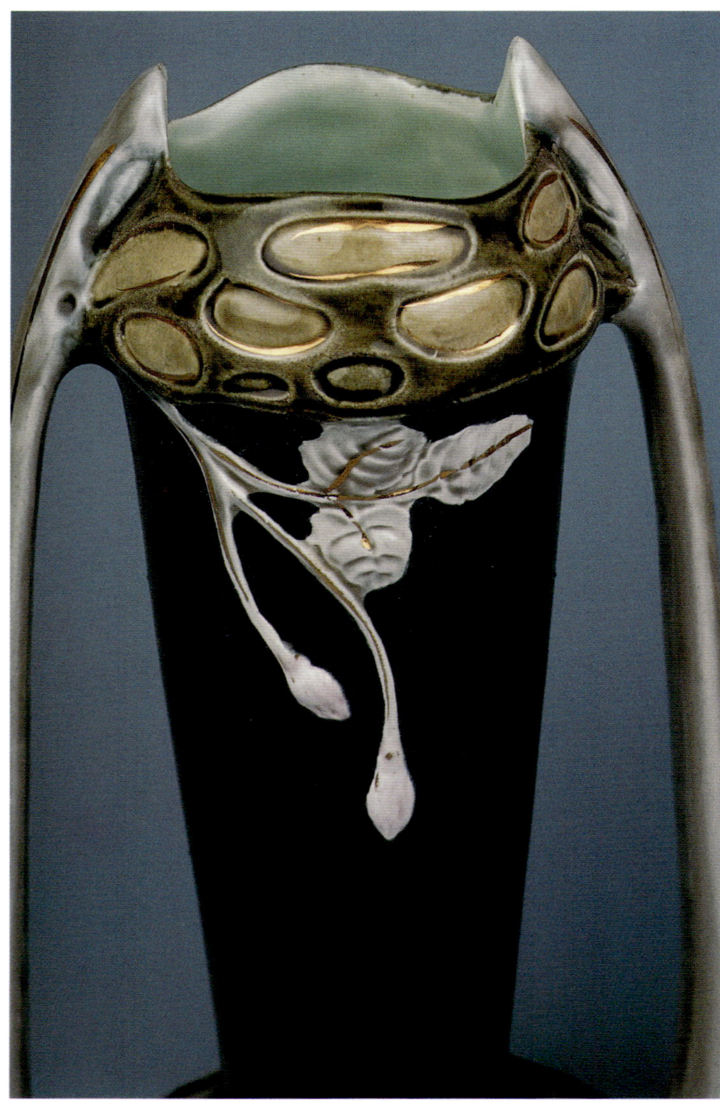

While the Arts and Crafts Movement rebelled against the industrialization and lowering of social values in Victorian society, Art Nouveau (1890-1914) railed against the Victorian penchant for designing objects steeped in the antiquarian's historicism (pulling designs and motifs from the ancients and applying them to new wares) – that common trend in early majolica ceramics introduced in the 1850s. Gardens, both the large public and small private varieties, were extremely popular in the Victorian age. Art Nouveau designers looked to the gardens and the natural world beyond for their inspiration. The results were decorative wares taking their forms from nature rather than history. Straight-lined precision symmetry was replaced with asymmetrical, sinuous, botanical ... and even faunal ... forms.

The Art Nouveau Movement also recognized the stressful nature of the urban lifestyle. It was believed that an interior space decorated in the Art Nouveau style would offer a restful place, providing the peace of nature to all who resided there. Therefore, the home or public space adorned in the Art Nouveau style would be therapeutic to the frazzled nerves of modern humanity.

Majolica's Manufacturers

Putti shell carriers on cobalt rimmed base, Minton, 11" w., 11" h. $6,000+.

In Britain

The majolica wares that graced homes were produced in England, Europe, and the United States. It all began in England's famous Staffordshire potting district with that collaboration of Herbert Minton and Jean François Léon Arnoux. Following the success of the Crystal Palace Exhibition, noted both for the purchase of Minton's majolica vases by the Crown Princess of Prussia and the general excitement over majolica among consumers and other potters, Herbert Minton maintained a touring stock of impressive majolica items guaranteed to continue to pique the interest of consumers and competitors alike. With his touring stock, Minton's firm maintained a presence at international exhibitions throughout the 1850s and the following decades. This presence served the firm well, generating interest at home and abroad in these brightly colored and creatively designed wares. In 1855, Minton's firm was awarded the *Legion d'Honneur* by Napoleon III for the majolica wares exhibited at the Universal Exhibition in Paris. Minton's majolica production ranged from ornate decorative items and massive garden ornaments to useful dishes and pitchers for dining rooms and kitchen use. By the time of Herbert Minton's death in 1858, the company was recognized as one of the largest decorative ceramic manufacturers in the western world.

Minton & Company placed an advertisement in the *Art Journal* in 1862, enumerating the wares the company had on display at the International Exhibition in London that year. The advertisement stated,

> The house of "Minton & Co." of Stoke-upon-Trent is renowned not only in Great Britain but over the World: its fame was established in 1851, and is fully sustained in 1862. ... The Italian Vase is Majolica, decorated from a design by Mr. Alfred Stevens.

Of Staffordshire

The English pottery manufacturers discussed here were established in the Staffordshire potting district. Located in the center of the country, the Staffordshire region contained a variety of rich clays, high quality coal, and reasonable access to transportation routes. In time, a canal would be dug to support the pottery industry in Staffordshire, later replaced by railroad lines. To the locals, the district was referred to simply as "The Potteries." Boroughs, townships, and villages included within the Staffordshire pottery district were Burslem, Brownhills, Cobridge, Etruria, Fenton, Hanley, Lane Delph, Lane End, Longport, Longton, Shelton, Stoke-Upon-Trent, and Tunstall. By 1841, this important industry employed approximately 20,000 individuals.

A term well known to today's drivers may have originated with an annoying habit of potters in "The Potteries" prior to 1700. These early ceramists, looking for a quick and easy source of clay, dug holes in Staffordshire roadways. In time, these holes became known as ... "potholes."

The venerable Wedgwood pottery company (Staffordshire, c. 1759-present) entered the majolica market in 1862. By 1880, the Wedgwood designs had diverged from Minton's. Majolica tablewares were their specialties; the firm was almost unrivaled in their production of useful majolica for the dining room and around the house. So admired were Wedgwood's majolica designs and glazes among Europeans that many Continental potters imitated Wedgwood's wares.

Classical style lion footed comport with water lily reticulated top, Wedgwood, 9"d., 5.5"h. $675-750 each.

Argenta sunflower and urn pitcher, Wedgwood, 8" h. $550-600.

The 1870s proved to be a peak period of majolica production for Wedgwood. Japanese designs were popular during this period, and Wedgwood produced a formal, sparsely decorated majolica "Argenta" line to meet the public's demand for Japanese decorative motifs. Argenta featured limited, colorfully glazed molded relief decoration that contrasted well with an off-white body. Wedgwood continued to manufacture majolica on into the twentieth century, in greatly reduced quantities that reflected the sharp drop in demand.

A Cautionary Note to Collectors: The Other "Wedgwoods!"

There are quite a few nineteenth century ceramic pieces featuring the name Wedgwood as *part* of their manufacturers' marks that are the products of pottery firms unrelated to the famous manufactory established by Josiah Wedgwood. Collectors should keep in mind that the Wedgwood pottery firm discussed to this point never added "& Co." to the Wedgwood name. Nor did they use the initial "J" preceding the Wedgwood name, or misspell the family name as either "Wedgewood" or "Vedgwood." The firm never marked their pieces "Wedgwood Ware" or "Queen's Ware." All of these marks have been employed by other firms. The collector, dealer, or auctioneer who is unclear on these points will make mistakes.

Ralph Wedgwood was manufacturing a variety of pottery wares, including creamware, as early as 1793. He marked his wares "Wedgwood & Co." with either impressed or printed marks. In 1798, he partnered with the firm William Tomlinson & Company at the Knottingly Pottery in Yorkshire, England, and continued there until 1801. The partners decided the "Wedgwood & Co." mark would carry more weight, dropping the Tomlinson name from their marks. In 1801, Ralph Wedgwood dissolved the partnership. That put an end to the first use of the "Wedgwood & Co." mark.

The pottery company Podmore, Walker & Company, manufacturing a variety of ceramics from 1834 to 1859, picked up the "Wedgwood & Co." mark. The reason for this was that the partner who comprised the "& Company" in the firm's title was Enoch Wedgwood. In 1860, the company name was changed to Wedgwood & Company (Ltd.) and the firm continued to manufacture pottery under that title and mark until 1965. Please remember that neither Josiah Wedgwood nor any of the various managers who have been in charge of Josiah Wedgwood's firm since ever added "& Co." to any of their marks. Josiah Wedgwood's firm used two simple name marks, either "Wedgwood" or "Wedgwoods."

Located in Stockton-on-Tees, England, one company employed a variety of obviously misleading marks to entice people to buy their wares, trading on several unusual variations of the famous Wedgwood name. William Smith & Company used the following marks: "Wedgewood," "Vedgwood," "Wedgwood Ware," and "Queen's Ware." They also used one honest mark, featuring the company's actual initials: "W.S. & Co." This mark was most likely employed after an injunction was filed against the firm, prohibiting them from using any variation of the Wedgwood name again. William Smith & Company was in business from 1825 to 1855.

Finally, there is one other firm whose mark causes confusion. John Wedg Wood produced ceramics in abundance. His wares were well made and followed the American pioneers as they moved westward across the plains of the expanding United States. There is quite a lot of his company's pottery to be found on the antiques market today. John Wedg Wood used the following marks (which frequently cause confusion among collectors today, and no doubt worked in his favor with consumers of his day as well): "J. WEDG. WOOD" or "WEDG WOOD". Note the space between the G and the W. John Wedg Wood ran his company from 1848 to 1857. His brother, Edmund T. Wood, continued the firm's pottery production until 1875. Edmund Wood used a "WEDGEWOOD & CO." mark.

So look closely at the mark on the back of that Wedgwood pot. Be sure you know *which* Wedgwood you are dealing with!

Overlapping ferns and leaves platter with twig handles, George Jones, 14" l. This beautiful platter sold at auction in 2004 for $2,300.

The talented potter George Jones apprenticed with Minton in the 1850s. Following the establishment of his own pottery factory, George Jones & Sons Ltd. (Stoke-on-Trent, Staffordshire, 1861-1907), Jones soon rivaled Minton in the production of quality majolica items. George Jones focused on the production of useful, rather than ornamental, wares, including ashtrays, footed centerpieces, cheese domes, caviar servers, oyster plates, platters, sardine boxes, place card stands, and spittoons.

Among George Jones & Sons' more popular patterns were "Dogwood," "Dogwood and Woven Fence," and "Iris and Lily." The firm also became well-known for the use of English birds in their decorations, and for their penchant for humorous pieces. As demand for majolica declined in England in the 1880s, however, George Jones & Sons largely turned to the production of other wares.

Iris and lily cobalt pitcher, George Jones, 5" h. $2,660-2,930.

George Jones & Sons became well known for their penchant for humorous majolica pieces. "Mr. Punch" punch bowl with turquoise ground, George Jones, hard to find in turquoise, 11" d., 8.25" h. Mr. Punch's estimated value is approximately $9,000-9,900. In 2004, however, this punch bowl sold at auction for $16,500.

One common characteristic of much of George Jones' majolica is the glazing of the bases of his wares with a distinctive green and brown tortoiseshell pattern. It is interesting to note that a large American majolica producer, Griffen, Smith & Company, also chose to decorate the bases of some of their majolica wares with a tortoiseshell glaze.

Other well-known English pottery firms producing majolica included Brown-Westhead, Moore & Company (Shelton, Hanley, Staffordshire, c. 1862-1904), W.T. Copeland & Sons (Stoke-on-Trent, Staffordshire, 1847-1970), Simon Fielding & Company (Stoke, Staffordshire, 1879 onward), and Joseph Holdcroft (Longton, Staffordshire, 1865-1939). In 1882, the Thomas Forester pottery firm (Thomas Forester, Longton, Staffordshire, 1877-1883; Thomas Forester & Son(s) (Ltd.), Longton, Staffordshire, c. 1884-1959) advertised low-priced majolica wares in the *Pottery Gazette*. Among the wares listed and displayed were basket vases, candle holders, comports, flowerpots, footed console bowls, pedestaled jardinières, match safes with strikers, mounted teapots, pitchers (including gurgling fish pitchers), sardine dishes, spittoons, strawberry sets, toy services, and vases with dolphin bases. In the *Pottery Gazette* in 1886, the firm William Brownfield & Son (Cobridge, Staffordshire, 1850-1892) advertised their wares, listing majolica among their "useful and ornamental goods." Wares displayed in the Brownfield & Son advertisement included ewer and basin wash sets, plates, and tureens.

Above and right:
W. T. Copeland & Sons ewer with putti angel faces and birds in high relief, band of ivy and berries on cobalt ground, 10.5" h. $2,500+.

S. Fielding & Co. (Ltd.) (Stoke, Staffordshire, England, 1879 onward) bird and fan turquoise cup and saucer. $250-300.

Joseph Holdcroft's rare double shell owl server; it is rare with the owl center handle, 16" l., 8.5" h. $5,000+.

Thomas Forester's (Longton, Staffordshire, England, 1877-1883; Thomas Forester & Son(s) (Ltd.), Longton, Staffordshire, England, c. 1884-1959) stork and cattail flower vase, 10.5" h. $500-550.

Left and right: William Brownfield's (& Son(s) Cobridge, Staffordshire, England, 1850-1892) ram's head ewer with ribbon and drapes of leaves and roses in high relief, 14" h. $1,800-1,980.

On the Continent

French Palissy style planter with fish, leaves and ferns, unmarked, 7" w., 5.5" h. $2,640+.

Following the Paris and London Exhibitions of 1855 and 1862, European potters from France, Germany, Austria, Central Europe, the Scandinavian countries, and Portugal all began producing majolica. Some European potters produced majolica in the English style while others turned to their own Renaissance antiquities (taking inspiration from the naturalistic work of Bernard Palissy (1510-1590), the French potter whose ceramics had adorned grottoes for Catherine de Medici) for inspiration and design. The potteries in France, Germany, and Austria were the most likely to produce majolica based on English designs, with the largest quantities emanating from the Sarreguemines factory in Lorraine, France.

In France

Pair of dolphin and shell vases by Sarreguemines (Sarreguemines, France, 1780-present), shape no. 949, 14.5" h. $1,600+ pair.

In 1780, Sarreguemines was established by entrepreneurs from Strasburg, Joseph Fabry and brothers Paul-Augustin Jacobi and Nicolas-Henri Jacobi. François-Paul Utzschneider gained control of the Sarreguemines factories, large pottery works at Digion and Limoges in the Lorraine region of France (and following the Franco-Prussian War of 1870 in Prussia). So impressed with the company's work was Napoléon, that he awarded Paul Utzschneider the Legion of Honour. In the 1850s, the company's principle product was faïence, a French tin-glazed earthenware. Expansion in the 1860s (there were four Sarreguemines factories by 1869), and Europe's increasing interest in majolica following the exhibitions of 1855 and 1862, led the company to produce a wide variety of majolica wares. With kilns designed by Léon Arnoux (ordered from the Minton factory and installed in the new works at the Digion plant) Sarreguemines began producing majolica following English designs. The company was also known for their production of fine stonewares.

The Digion factory became the largest of its type in France, supporting over 2,000 workers and creating majolica of a quality rivaling Minton's. Sarreguemines manufactured majolica into the early twentieth century, maintaining a high standard of quality to the end. The firm produced some striking solid green glazed majolica oyster plates.

It is worth noting that in 1997, the Vitry-Le-François, Digion, Manufacture of Lunéville-Saint-Clément, and Sarreguemines pottery works joined forces to create the "Group Sarreguemines." Between them, the firms currently produce decorative tablewares and gift wares, hotel porcelain, sanitary wares, and floor tiles. The decorative tablewares and gift wares are produced by the Manufacture of Lunéville-Saint-Clément and the floor tiles are produced by Sarreguemines.

Choisy-le-Roi was established in France as a faïence pottery in 1804. In the early 1860s, like Sarreguemines, Choisy-le-Roi added majolica to their production and would continue manufacturing majolica wares until 1910. While fascination with Renaissance design strongly influenced the firm's majolica design in the early 1860s, the inclusion of Japanese ceramics at the Paris exhibitions of 1867 and 1878 brought Oriental design sensibilities to Choisy. Asymmetrical designs based on Japanese motifs dominated at Choisy during this period. Other decorative motifs employed by the firm during the last quarter of the nineteenth century included a variation on shell-and-seaweed patterns and leaf plates.

La Faïencerie d'Onnaing of northern France produced majolica in abundance. Theirs were largely examples of the later, inexpensive majolica wares produced for the novelty export market. Onnaing majolica was made from 1870 to World War I, and again after the war until 1938. Among their majolica wares were candlestick holders, children's toys, small clocks, flowerpots, vases, umbrella stands, smoking accessories, and dinnerwares. Their tobacco jars, match strikers, and ashtrays were molded in a variety of whimsical forms including bears, devils, dragons, frogs, and vultures.

Two brothers, Delphin and Clément Massier, and their cousin Jérôme, began majolica production in 1860 in Vallauris in the south of France. The Messiers are known for their experimentation with glaze colors, broadening the majolica color range significantly. Among the notable artists working for them were Jean Barol and Jacques Sicard. Both Barol and Sicard were recognized for their iridescent glaze techniques. Sicard would go on to work for Weller Pottery in the United States during the early years of the twentieth century.

"Chante Clair" figural rooster pitcher by La Faïencerie d'Onnaing (Valenciennes, France, 1821-1894; in 1894 the company combines with Nimy to form the Onnaing Society, which continues to produce majolica until 1938), 9" h. These pitchers were produced during the First World War and used by children to collect money for wounded soldiers. This is the second of two versions, dating to c. 1914. The earlier version read "Vive la Russie" rather than "Le Gaulois" on the side. $300-540 depending on the phrase employed.

Among the Massier's most striking majolica wares were life-sized flamingos and roosters designed by Delphin Messier. Messier designs include Art Nouveau examples from the later production years, prior to the closure of the firm in the early twentieth century.

Large pink flamingo figural planter, Delphin Massier (Vallauris, France), 14.5" l., 10.5" h. $3,000-4,000.

The firm of Keller and Guerin (Lunéville, France, c. 1790-1892; Keller, Guerin & St. Clément, c. 1892 onward) produced a small amount of majolica at the historic Lunéville works. Their majolica used brilliant colors, heavy in blues and greens. Tea and coffee services, asparagus services, and accessory pieces were a specialty at Lunéville. Majolica production ceased in 1914. In about 1892, the firm changed its name to Keller, Guerin & St. Clément. In 1922, the Fenal family, owners and operators of the nearby Badonviller china factory, purchased the Luneville-St. Clément factories. The company name became the Société Anonyme, with pottery factories in Luneville, Badonviller, and St. Clément.

In Rimbaud, Belgium, Emile Lhermine founded a faïence pottery works in 1879. The firm was successful and began to expand in 1886. In time, the firm opened another factory across the Belgian border in Orchies, France. In 1923, Orchies purchased the Moulin des Loups & Hamages pottery works in the nearby town of St. Amand-les-Eaux.

Asparagus plate by Keller & Guerin (Lunéville, France, c. 1790-1892), 9". $200-300.

Among the wares produced at Orchies were a limited number of majolica figural jugs, oyster plates, a wide variety of utilitarian and table wares, and a line of luxury hand painted wares. The company would remain in operation until 1988.

Cat playing the mandolin pitcher, Orchies (Orchies, France, c. 1886-1988), 9.25" h. $435-535.

Majolica production at the Saint Clément firm began in the 1860s and continued for more than forty years. Majolica produced there included table and dessert services, asparagus-artichoke services, pitchers, and ornamental vases. Their majolica was by and large delicate in relief and subtle in shading. Outside of their usual line of majolica, Saint Clément also produced jardinières featuring Palissy-style decorations (that French style featuring very realistic animals, fish, insects, and plant life swarming over the surfaces of the wares).

In Central Europe, Germany, and Scandinavia

Three firms from Bohemia are known for their majolica production: Wilhelm Schiller and Son; Julius Dressler; and B. Bloch and Company. Of the three, Wilhelm Schiller and Son was the most prolific. Established in 1829 (then Schiller and Gerbing—the Wilhelm Schiller and Son name would not be adopted until 1885), Schiller began producing majolica wares in the 1860s. The company's majolica was well modeled and featured darker glaze color combinations characteristic of Central Europe.

Rooster pitcher by St. Clément (Lunéville, France), 11", $595-655.

Schiller specialized in decorative majolica, including some very impressive ornamental vases, centerpieces, ewers, pedestaled jardinières, wall plaques, and wall pockets. However, the firm also manufactured more practical wares, including candlesticks, card trays, humidors, lamps, matchboxes, pitchers, sardine boxes, and steins.

With the threat of the First World War looming over Europe, Wilhelm Schiller and Son ceased production and closed the factory.

Julius Dressler established his pottery, dedicated to the manufacture of majolica and porcelain, at roughly the same time as the Schiller firm launched their majolica lines (1860s). Dressler's company produced decorative serving wares including asparagus and berry sets, along with egg platters. Dressler would cease majolica production around 1910, although the firm would continue ceramics production until 1945.

B. Bloch and Company was founded in 1871, in part to take advantage of the popularity of majolica. The firm was one of the few that would continue majolica production into the 1930s. B. Bloch and Company's early majolica wares included smoking accessories for pipes and cigars. Among them were elaborate smoker's companions, which combined a cigar holder, match holder, striker, and occasionally a receptacle for burnt matches.

B. Bloch and Company also made extravagant ewers and centerpieces for which they became well known. Figural animal bottles were also among the company's repertoire. Heading into the twentieth century, the firm dropped much of the Victorian ornamentation and produced largely useful and inexpensive majolica wares, including baskets, bowls, cachepots, and sconces.

The largest German majolica manufacturer was Villeroy and Boch (Mettlach and other European locations, 1836-present). From roughly the 1850s to 1900, the firm generated prodigious quantities of majolica, including leaf plates and other tableware items reminiscent of English designs. Since the majority of Villeroy and Boch majolica was headed to the United States, and American consumers were known to favor British ceramics, emulating En-

Picket fence mottled sardine box with fish on cover, attached undertray by Wilhelm Schiller and Sons (W.S. & S., Bohemia; 1829 established as Schiller and Gerbing, 1885 name change to Wilhelm Schiller and Son, majolica production begins in the 1860s, firm closes c. First World War). $1,500-1,700.

Man with baskets match striker (match holder), by B. Bloch & Co., 10.5" h. $750-825.

glish design was wise business strategy. After 1900, the firm created a souvenir majolica line. Prior to the mid-twentieth century, long-distance travel was difficult at best. Souvenirs were held in higher esteem as a result, proving the owner had both the fortitude and resources for journeys far from home.

Georg Schneider was another notable German majolica manufacturer, producing majolica wares from c. 1890 to 1920. The company created both useful majolica lines in the English style and majolica souvenir items. Most common among their majolica wares were dessert plates. Ornamental majolica was left to other firms.

Noted for majolica figures was the Haldensleben, Germany, firm of Hugo Lonitz. Established in 1868, the company produced a variety of majolica figures depicting birds or humans. Several examples are found in this text. The factory added "& Co." to their name from 1886 to 1904.

Most of the majolica emanating from Scandinavia was produced by the Arabia Pottery, founded outside Helsinki, Finland, in 1874. A subsidiary company to Rörstrand Pottery of Sweden, Arabia produced large and functional majolica plant stands and jardinières in the Art Nouveau style.

In Portugal

Palissy style plaque with a snake, lizard, and other creatures on a bed of heavy grass by José A. Cunha, Portugal, 9.5" d. $1,320-1,450.

Portuguese pottery firms producing majolica and Palissy-style wares included José A. Cunha; Mafra and Son; The Manufacture Royale de Rato; and Rafael Bordalo Pinheiro. With the exception of The Manufacture Royale de Rato (Lisbon), all were located in Caldas da Rainha. Of these firms, Mafra and Son produced the vast majority of the Palissy-style wares (beginning in 1853) while José A. Cunha was well known around 1900 for majolica tableware items in imaginatively designed leaf forms. The Manufacture Royale de Rato was both a significant producer of majolica and an exhibitor of Palissy-style ware in the Paris Exhibition of 1867. Rafael Bordalo Pinheiro (1883 onward) manufactured a diverse range of majolica tiles, examples of which were on display at the Paris Exhibition of 1889.

In the United States

Oak leaf tray with pink border, Griffen, Smith & Co., 12.25". $565-625.

For centuries, American potters had been unable to compete against the long established potteries of England. Over time, a bias developed among American consumers: they believed that English pottery was far superior to anything an upstart American potter could create. The struggling American artisans felt that the Centennial Exhibition of 1876 in Philadelphia, Pennsylvania, offered them their best chance to change the minds of America's consumers. Some potters, Edwin Bennett, James Carr, and J. E. Jeffords among them, felt that majolica was the proper ware to display American potting prowess. Americans in the thousands saw the "home-grown" majolica and were impressed. The Centennial Exhibition did for majolica potters in the United States what the Crystal Palace Exhibition had done for Herbert Minton a quarter century earlier. As a result, the decade of the 1880s would see high demand for majolica wares in the United States. In fact, the 1880s would be a most colorful decade. Along with majolica, advances in lithography were creating color advertising and packaging found to be most impressive by American consumers.

Majolica at the Centennial Exhibition in 1876

A souvenir from a distant place or significant event meant more in the Victorian world. To have tangible evidence that you had both the financial resources and physical endurance to travel long distances in an age when travel was difficult in every way and most never strayed too far from home was considered quite impressive. An 1876 Centennial Exhibition jug with the busts of Washington and Lincoln on each side by Wedgwood, cobalt accent, 5.5". $1,250+.

Of course, American potters were not alone in displaying majolica to the public in 1876. British and French potteries were displaying majolica wares as well. Susan N. Carter expressed her opinions on the overseas majolica in a column for *Appleton's Journal* in July of 1876. She stated,

> Chief in the prominence which excellence and great numbers of articles give, are the English wares of Doulton and Minton; and tiles of every pattern, glazed and unglazed, Moorish and South Kensington, and those that compose into mediaeval designs, natural objects or pictured landscapes or genre scenes, are to be found. Their faience too is admirable; and, when we turn from it to look at that of Limoges, of Gien, and Loiret, in France, the Bernard Palissy faience, we perceive, for the first time, that all of them alike have the same sincere and simple interpretations of Nature well conventionalized, and that there is a similarity of genius between sturdy English character and a portion of the French nation, which made the latter Huguenots and genuine upholders of the Renaissance, and which has no affinities with the other portion of France represented by the customs and the art of Louis XIV and Louis XV. (1876, 74-77)

The original inspiration for majolica was also on display in 1876. The trade journal *Manufacturer and Builder* reported in November 1876,

> The most interesting collection of majolica [maiolica] is undoubtedly that now on exhibition at our Exhibition in Philadelphia; it is the private property of Mr. Castellani of Rome, and includes wares produced by the Arabs during their domination of Sicily, made in 1300-1400; Della Robbia ware of about 1450; Tuscan ware of 1470-1523; Siena ware of 1600; Castel Durante, Faenza, Romagna; etc., in all, some 400 to 500 specimens, which compete with one another in interest and beauty. (1876, 257)

Apparently unaware of ancient maiolica's role as inspiration for Minton's majolica (or unimpressed with the modern results to date), the anonymous reporter for *Manufacturer and Builder* states,

> ...its study by our artisans will certainly improve their taste, and be a stimulus for higher efforts when they see what the Italians produced four centuries ago. (1876, 257)

Not everyone exposed to the modern majolica displayed at the Centennial Exhibition was enthralled. Charles Wyllys Elliott made his feelings clear in *The Atlantic Monthly* in November 1876. He stated, unequivocally,

> Within a decade a kind of bold decorative pottery has appeared in England and elsewhere, and is called "majolica," for what reason one cannot divine. Some very large vases and pots of this work are to be seen in the Main Building, exhibited, we think, by Daniels and Son. The work seems a sort of cross between the Italian maiolicas and the Palissy ware. It does not attempt fineness or delicacy of form, or subtlety of color or meaning in its decoration; and indeed it is not possible to understand why it should be. But it has for the last ten years been largely produced and widely sold, and it must gratify a certain want. Who buys it and where it goes, who can tell? For in these ten years the writer has seen but one piece of it in any house except a hotel. Is it true that the people who go to hotels and who travel in steamboats demand this sort of thing? Is it indeed true that whatever is bad and big finds its pedestal in those palaces because their patrons cry for them; or is it that the designers of these caravansaries suppose they do, and are frightfully mistaken? Or is it possible that what no one else will buy a hotel-manager always does? Of this class of work the best we saw in the collection of Rostrand of Stockholm, and has the merit of good and quiet color. (1876, 572)

Despite Mr. Elliott's protestations, majolica was wildly popular in the United States during the following decade.

Immigrant British potters William and Edwin Bennett established the E. & W. Bennett pottery in Baltimore, Maryland, in 1848. With William's departure, the name changed to the Edwin Bennett Pottery in 1856. Having displayed his majolica during the Centennial Exhibition, Bennett would go on to produce majolica wares during the 1880s, when demand for majolica in America was at its height. The Bennett factory was the largest pottery firm in the Baltimore area and remained active until c. 1937.

James Carr arrived in the United States from England in 1844. He had worked with well-known British potters James Clews and John Ridgway prior to his arrival. By 1853, Carr had established his own pottery works, the New York City Pottery, in Manhattan. In the years to come, Carr would train many American potters who would go on to successfully produce majolica, including J. E. Jeffords.

Majolica wares were added to Carr's high-quality product line in the mid-1860s. Included among his majolica offerings was a combination of the useful and the ornamental, including centerpieces, comports, game dishes, garden seats, match strikers, pitchers, sardine boxes, and vases. Best known among Carr's majolica was a line decorated in a cauliflower motif similar to a Wedgwood design. It is not surprising, in fact, that English designs and techniques were often used in the creation of Carr's majolica.

Majolica from the New York City Pottery won awards at both the Philadelphia Centennial Exhibition in 1876 and the Paris Exposition of 1878. Carr's firm would continue to produce majolica wares until 1888, when the factory closed.

Once trained by James Carr, J. E. Jeffords founded his Philadelphia City Pottery in 1868. Jeffords was well known for casting unusually large pottery. The public's attention was quickly captured by his twenty gallon teapot, complete with a four foot high majolica pedestal, featured at the Centennial Exhibition. Jeffords' Philadelphia City Pottery would continue producing majolica and other wares until the factory ceased production in 1890.

While Griffen, Smith & Company, originally Griffen, Smith & Hill, was not among the first American potteries to produce majolica, many ceramics historians have considered the firm one of the best and most prolific. Established in an existing pottery factory in Phoenixville, Pennsylvania, in 1879 by American brothers Henry and George Griffen, William Hill, and English potter, David Smith, the firm began producing majolica in 1882. While William Hill had left the firm by the time majolica production began, and the name had changed from Griffen, Smith & Hill to Griffen, Smith & Company, the company's manufacturer's mark continued to carry the GSH monogram familiar to majolica collectors.

Having missed the Centennial Exhibition in Philadelphia, Griffen, Smith & Company took advantage of the World's Industrial and Cotton Centennial Exposition in New Orleans in 1884. Here they won critical acclaim and, with the help of a colorful catalog of their majolica wares printed for the occasion, captured the attention of the American public.

Examples of Griffen, Smith & Co. (originally Griffen Smith & Hill) (Phoenixville, Pennsylvania, 1879-1889) majolica. **Left:** Overlapping begonia leaf plate, 9". **Right:** Strawberry and apple basket weave plate with cobalt rim, 9.25" d. **Left:** $375-415. **Right:** $715-790.

The familiar GSH monogram is found in the center of the Griffen, Smith & Co. manufacturer's mark. The company gave their majolica the trade name Etruscan as Etruscan antiquities were fascinating the American public at that time.

Two Geranium platters, Griffen, Smith & Co., 12". $350-385 each.

Shell and seaweed platter, Griffen, Smith & Co., 14". $1,450-1,600.

Griffen, Smith & Company's 1884 Catalog Listings

Here is a list of Griffen, Smith & Company's 1884 majolica wares and the decorative motifs adorning them.

- Ashtray in Begonia and Butterfly pattern.
- Basket in Begonia; Wicker patterns.
- Berry Tray in Cosmos (Conventional [this was a stylized floral pattern]) pattern.
- Bowl & Plate in Cauliflower pattern.
- Bowl in Bamboo pattern.
- Bowl in Cauliflower pattern.
- Bowls (low & high) in Lily pattern.
- Bowls (low & high) in Rose pattern.
- Box & Stand in Sardine pattern.
- Bread Tray in Oak pattern.
- Cake Stand in Conventional pattern.
- Cake tray in Geranium; Napkin patterns.
- Card comport in Morning Glory pattern.
- Card Trays in Oak pattern (including leaves and branches)
- Celery in unnamed pattern.
- Cigar Box in Shell & Seaweed pattern.
- Comport in Dolphin pattern.
- Comport in Grape Leaf pattern.
- Comports in Maple pattern.
- Covered Butter in Bamboo pattern.
- Covered Butter in Butterfly pattern.
- Covered Cheese in Lily pattern.
- Cream in Bamboo pattern.
- Cream in Bird pattern.
- Cup & saucer in Bamboo pattern.
- Cuspidor in Lily; Pineapple patterns.
- Cuspidor in Sunflower pattern.
- Flower Pot in Fern and Floral pattern.
- Fruit in Smilax; Cosmos (Conventional); Begonia on Wicker; Bird patterns.
- Fruit Tray in Oak pattern.
- Individual berry tray with cream and sugar in Strawberry pattern.
- Individual butter dishes in Lily; Leaf on Plate; Begonia Leaf; Geranium Leaf; Smilax; Pansy; and Wicker & Begonia patterns.
- Individual salt in Swan pattern.
- Jug in Corn pattern.
- Jug in Sunflower pattern.
- Jug in Thorn pattern.
- Jugs in Straight; Rustic; Rose; Conventional; Corn; Baseball & Soccer; Fern patterns.
- Mug in Lily pattern.
- Mug in Oak pattern.
- Nappy in Shell & Seaweed pattern.
- Paperweight in Swan pattern.
- Pin Tray in Leaf pattern.
- Plate for bowl in Rose pattern.
- Plates in Leaf on Plate; Begonia; Maple Leaves; Lily (Conventional); Bamboo; Cauliflower patterns.
- Salad comport in Daisy pattern.
- Salad in Lily pattern.
- Sardine Box in Lily & Swan pattern.
- Sauce Dish in Daisy pattern.
- Soap in Oak
- Spice Tray in Leaves pattern.
- Spooner in Bamboo pattern.
- Spooner in Bird pattern.
- Sugar in Bird pattern.
- Teapot in Bamboo pattern.
- Teapot in Bird pattern.
- Teapot in Cauliflower pattern.
- Teapot stand in Conventional pattern.
- Tray in Begonia and Wicker.
- Trays in Begonia Leaf; Leaf patterns.
- Vase in Lily pattern.
- Vase in Lion pattern.
- Vase in Oak pattern.
- Vase, small, in Corn pattern. (Weidner 1960)

Large as this listing is, it by no means represents the entire output of Griffen, Smith & Company majolica. Other forms with different decorative motifs will be found throughout this book.

During the 1884 Exposition in New Orleans, Griffen, Smith & Company's majolica came to the attention of the management of the Great Atlantic and Pacific Tea Company (the A & P), a rising power in retail sales. An agreement was reached and small majolica items from the company were soon offered as A & P premiums across the nation.

The vast majority of the majolica wares produced by this prolific firm were useful in nature, including bowls, butter pats, comports, covered dishes, plates, platters, tea sets, and tobacco jars. Wide ranging decorative motifs were employed. Like Choisy-le-Roi in France, shell-and-seaweed, leaf patterns (a single Begonia leaf design used for pickle dishes and pin trays was popular), and Japanese asymmetrical motifs (most often including either birds or bamboo in the decoration) were used to good effect. Also produced were wares featuring sunflowers, vegetables, additional foliage of all sorts, and a variety of popular British motifs (including "Albino" majolica featuring a Japanese-style motif—basically a white background glaze adorned with minimal molded and colored glazed border decoration similar to Wedgwood's Argenta). The bamboo motif was a favorite with many American majolica manufacturers in the 1880s. Griffen, Smith & Company produced a wide selection of bamboo adorned bowls, cream pitchers, sugar bowls, teapots, and spooners.

At the time Griffin, Smith and Company was producing majolica, there was significant public interest in Etruscan revivalist decorative arts. The firm promptly christened their majolica "Etruscan." The name harkened back to the potters of ancient Rome in the last seven centuries B.C., grounding the company's increasingly popular modern ware in the romance of the distant past. Minton had done just the same thing a quarter century before them.

In 1889, David Smith was forced to retire in poor health. His shares in the business were sold to J. Stuart Love, Henry Griffen's father-in-law. The company name changed to Griffen, Love & Company. This sale curtailed any further serious majolica production in Phoenixville. In the winter of 1890, as interest in majolica was waning in the United States, a massive fire nearly destroyed the factory. While a number of lesser operators would use the site and continue to produce small amounts of majolica until c. 1902, the firm never truly recovered from the disastrous blaze.

Many other American potteries, both large and small, took to the production of majolica during the height of its popularity. Among their ranks were Arsenal Pottery (Trenton, New Jersey), The Chesapeake Pottery Company (Baltimore, Maryland), Eureka Pottery (Trenton, New Jersey), The Faience Manufacturing Company (Greenpoint, New York), The Hampshire Pottery (Keene, New Hampshire), Morley & Company (Wellsville and East Liverpool, Ohio), The New Milford Pottery Company (later the Wannopee Pottery Company, New Milford, Connecticut), Odell and Booth Brothers (Tarrytown, New York), Peekskill Pottery Company (Peekskill, New York), and Willets Manufacturing Company (Trenton, New Jersey).

Tri-corners owl and fan pitcher by Eureka Pottery (Trenton, New Jersey, 1883-1887), 7". $450-495.

Arsenal Pottery

The Arsenal Pottery of Trenton, New Jersey, did not generally mark their wares. This has led to many misidentifications, attributing this company's wares to other American or overseas firms. Arsenal was owned and operated from 1876 to 1905 by James and Joseph Mayer. They produced a variety of wares ranging from the useful (jugs [common nineteenth century terminology for "pitchers"] and plates) to the ornamental (jardinières and vases). In recent years, archaeologists surveying along the realignment path for New Jersey Route 29 discovered and excavated Arsenal Pottery's waster dump, recovering hundreds of majolica shards. True to form, these shards were largely unmarked. Glazes found on these artifacts were described as brightly colored polychromes including aqua, brown, dark blue, gray, green, natural white, pink, purple, red, and yellow-green. Gold gilt was in evidence and the interiors of hollow wares and the undersides of plates and platters featured pale glaze washes in cream, green, and pink. Some flat wares (plates, platters, etc.) were also decorated with brown sponged backgrounds.

These artifacts, described below, will assist archaeologists, dealers, auctioneers, and collectors alike in identifying the majolica wares produced by this elusive New Jersey firm.

Bowls:
- Cabbage bordered bowl with grape leaves in center, 8.25" (also made in 10").

Creamers:
- Tree bark motif with simple toothed leaf and ferns, 5.25" (also made in 8").
- Bamboo with daisies, 5".
- Multi-petal flower (possibly wild rose) over a basket weave background, 4.75" (also made in 8").

Jardinières:
- Jardinières, scales and scrolls in solid colors (blue, green, or yellow).

Jugs (a.k.a. Pitchers):
- Water lily flower with overlapping lily pads (handle has tadpole on top), 7".
- Green plant (no flower) on wooden barrel with wood hoops, rope pattern handle is flat in cross section, 6".
- Tree with bird's nest, eggs and bird (robin?) with branch handle, 9".
- Bark pitcher with wild rose with branch handle, 8.25" (also made in 6", 7", and 9.5").
- Bark pitcher with wild rose with branch handle, 7" (also made in 6").
- Figural pitcher/mug (Toby) of man's head with top hat (marked "PAT APLD FOR"), 4.75".
- Corn ear shaped pitcher.
- Pitcher with tree bark, grape vine, leaves, and grapes.
- Pitcher with scales and scrolls in solid colors (blue, green, or yellow).

Plates:
- Hounds chasing elk or deer through grass with floral scroll and geometric border, 8" (also made in 9", 9.5", and 11" diameter.)
- Center toby scene (a man with a pitcher and mug in either hand sitting on a keg [see *Majolica: British, American, & European Wares*, p. 139, for a similar item]) surrounded by a raised shell and dot diaper border and scrolling rim, 10".
- Sheepdog in front of doghouse and dog bowl with leaf and scroll border, 10.75".
- Wild rose and three simple toothed leaves on basket weave background, 9.25" (also made in 8").
- Fish-shaped plate with scales and fins (polychrome), 12.5" x 6.5". *Note: this plate has been reproduced.
- Begonia leaf plate, 7.75" x 5.75".
- Girl and large dog in front of fireplace feeding rabbit a plate of lettuce with dot-diaper-scallop shell border.

Spittoons:
- Basket spittoon (with two varieties of bird on a branch on a basket and rose-bow on basket).

Teapots:
- Basket weave teapot lid, 4" diameter. (Liebeknecht August/September 2001)

In 1881, F. E. Fryatt, writing for *Harper's New Monthly Magazine*, described the setting in Trenton, New Jersey, where Arsenal Pottery was situated, as follows:

> Reaching the southern or eastern portion of the city, one is surrounded by telling signs of the peculiar activity which has appropriately given this region its title of the "Staffordshire of America." On every side may be seen smoking chimneys and kilns looming above tall modern factories, or long, low, weather-stained buildings, lumbering carts filled with raw material, and drays piled high with casks and crates of finished ware. (1881, 359)

Majolica's Manufacturers' Marks

Majolica wares were manufactured in abundance. Many potters, both the large and well known and the small and obscure, produced majolica. Many of the smaller potteries did not mark their wares; it did not profit them to identify themselves if they had no reputation to work with. On the other hand, at times small firms were able to purchase the worn molds featuring decorative motifs that were falling out of favor from larger establishments. It helped those small potteries if pieces they made from these old molds were mistaken for the wares of the larger and more prestigious firm.

This makes dating unmarked and unattributed majolica with anything approaching precision difficult at best. Many times the most you can hope for is to know the date of earliest possible production.

Minton impressed name mark and molded diamond-shaped registration mark. The impressed Minton name mark was in use from c. 1862-1872.

Mintons impressed name mark with year cipher. The addition of the "s" to the Minton impressed name mark was used from 1873-1951. The impressed mark above the M in Mintons is the year cipher for 1873, the N refers to the month of November, and the third mark should be the potter's mark. The number 1451 is a Minton company shape number code for internal use.

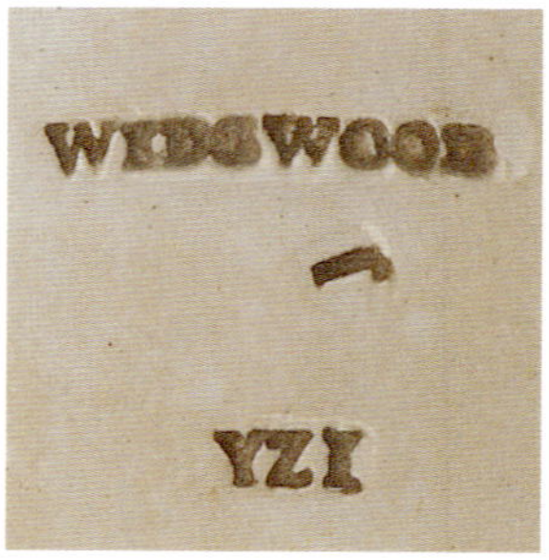

Impressed Wedgwood mark (in use in some form from the company's establishment in 1759 to the present) and three letter coding. The first letter indicates the month, the second the potter, and the third the year. In this case, the Y is May and the I is 1880. (For a complete listing of Minton and Wedgwood date coding, see Kowalsky 1999.)

Dating Majolica with Manufacturers' Marks

Majolica pieces from many British, American, and European pottery companies bear distinctive manufacturers' marks. The marks on majolica usually include the manufacturer's name and/or the symbol of the company and were applied in one of several ways. Some were impressed with a stamp into the soft earthenware bodies of unfired wares, as was the Minton name. Manufactur-

Impressed George Jones & Sons circular monogram mark, used from c. 1865-1877, with impressed registration mark. This registration mark was in use from 1868-1883, placing the day at the apex of the diamond below the circle, the year on the right in a single letter code (H in this case), and the month at the base of the diamond, also as a single letter code (A in this mark). The date of registration was December 22, 1869.

Molded George Jones & Sons manufacturer's mark with company initials monogram and location "Stoke-on-Trent" included. The G. J. monogram alone was in use from 1861 to 1873. The G. J. monogram appeared in this "blue pad" from c. 1865-1878.

Two impressed Griffen, Smith & Company GSH monogram manufacturer's marks (1879-1889), with and without the firm's Etruscan trade name in a circular band around the initials. The company began to offer majolica in 1882. The mark without the circular band is the earliest. The firm's original name was Griffen, Smith & Hill. William Hill left the company early but the monogram remained the same for quite a while.

ers' marks were also scratched into the unfired ware, painted on the surface before or after glazing, or applied as a transfer print, once again appearing either under or over the glaze.

These marks may be quite useful. Many large firms with long lives used a variety of marks over time. Each mark would come into use and then be dropped in favor of a new mark for any of a number of reasons including a name change to the firm when a new partner or a son came on board, when the company was incorporated, or when the firm changed location, to name just a few. As research continues into the history of these firms, it becomes more precisely known when a specific mark was used. By knowing the dates certain marks were used, a collector may tell at a glance roughly how old a particular piece is by the mark applied to it.

However, without knowing the history of a particular firm, but knowing when certain terms and/or symbols first appeared on specific marks, a great deal of information may be gleaned from the manufacturers' marks. The following guidelines provide key elements of English and American mark identification from the mid-nineteenth on through the mid-twentieth century.

1842-1883 *Registration marks* (see discussion below) came into use with manufacturers' marks in 1842 and ceased to be used after 1883. The diamond-shaped registration mark was an English designation indicating that a design or process had been registered.

1845 *Stafford Knot,* bow knot shape mark.

post-1850 *"Royal"* in the manufacturer's trade name was used on many English marks after 1850.

1859 *"Copyright"* indicates a design, name or material is registered under United States copyright laws from 1859 to the present. It is usually a 20th century mark.

The impressed manufacturer's mark "Frie Onnaing" of La Faïencerie d'Onnaing (producers of majolica from 1870 to 1900 from northern France). The company's more expensive wares received this manufacturer's mark. The lesser wares received only a three or four digit number code. This manufacturer's mark is accompanied by "Made in France" to comply with the 1891 McKinley Tariff Act, which demanded that foreign imports be marked with the country of origin.

1861 *"Limited"* or any standard abbreviation on English wares was incorporated into manufacturers' marks post-dating an 1855 act establishing them and this term does not actually appear in use before 1861.

post-1862, England; post-1875 U.S. *"Trade Mark"* has been applied to English pieces in accord with the Trademark Act of 1862 and was applied to American wares after 1875.

1877 *"Copyright Reserved"* on a mark dates from 1877 and is a legal term used on English wares.
post-1880 *"England"* in the mark indicates a date after 1880, and generally after 1891 on export wares.
1884 *Registration numbers* originate in 1884 (see below). They are an English designation which indicates that a design or process has been registered.
1887 *"Made In"* begins use in 1887 and continues to be used on wares imported to England. The British Merchandise Marks Act required imported wares to be marked with these words and the country name or with the country name alone. However, for pieces that were difficult to mark, it was sufficient to have the country of origin labeled on the package, if not on the piece. Therefore, it cannot be assumed that all pieces found without "Made In" marks date prior to the Act. Also, pieces produced for a country's home market would not receive this mark and could have traveled to other parts of the world later with immigrant families.
1890 *"Warranted"* was used in several ways. In the United States and England it appears as part of the company name in the 1890s.
1891 *Country of origin*, American McKinley Tariff Act requires imported wares to be marked with the country of origin.
1900 *"Patented"* occurs from 1900 onward. "Patented" signifies that a patent was granted by the United States Patent Office.
post-1901 *"U.S. patent"* was used after 1901 to denote that the design or method is patented in the United States. This term is also found on wares made outside the United States.
1902 *"Patent applied for"* dates from 1902 to the present. It signifies that a patent application has been filed with the United States Patent Office.
1927 *"Designed or Made Expressly For"* appears on British wares made specifically for a single client. Such items may be marked with the client's name and/or with the factory name.

When presented with majolica without marks, you need to rely on knowledge of the manufacturers and their patterns, vessel forms, and the general periods during which major social and artistic movements altered designs.

Registration Marks

English registration marks are possibly the most complete and useful marks for dating English majolica. Since 1842, English decorative art designs have been registered at the British patent office; however, not every registered piece is marked.

A diamond-shaped mark was used between 1842 and 1883. The information within the diamond changed after 1867. In 1884, the diamond-shaped marks were dropped in favor of simpler registry numbers (Rd. No.), indicating the year the piece was registered in a numeric sequence beginning in 1884 with the number 1. Registry numbers provide the earliest possible date of manufacture.

Impressed diamond-shaped Registration Mark. This registration mark was in use from 1868-1883, placing the day at the apex of the diamond below the circle, the year on the right in a single letter code (H in this case), and the month at the base of the diamond, also as a single letter code (A in this mark). The number to the left is the parcel number. The date of registration was December 22, 1869.

The diamond-shaped registry marks from 1842-1867 contain letters and numbers to indicate:

- the large Rd is an abbreviation for "registered,"
- the Roman numeral in the circle at the top of the mark represents the type of material from which the piece was produced,
- the letter in the top inside section of the diamond represents the year the piece was registered,
- the Arabic numeral in the right section represents the day of the month the piece was registered,
- the Arabic numeral in the section at the base represents the parcel number, which is a code indicating the person or company who registered the piece,
- and the letter in the left section represents the month the piece was registered.

From 1868-1883, the numbers and their locations were changed:

- the large Rd and Roman numeral above the diamond remain unchanged,
- the Arabic numeral in the top inside section of the diamond represents the day of the month the piece was registered,
- the letter in the right-hand section represents the year the piece was registered,
- the letter in the bottom section signifies the month the piece was registered,
- and the Arabic numeral in the left-hand section represents the parcel number.

The tables below provide the code numbers and letters on the diamond-shaped registry marks (for more information see Kowalsky 1999, 578-593).

TABLE 1: Type of material by class

Class I	Ornamental designs in metal
Class II	Ornamental designs in wood
Class III	Ornamental designs in glass
Class IV	**Ornamental designs in earthenware/ porcelain, ivory bone, and other solid substances**
Class V	Ornamental designs – Paper hangings
Class VI	Ornamental designs – Carpets, floor or oil cloth
Class VII	Ornamental designs – Shawls – printed patterns
Class VIII	Ornamental designs – Shawls – patterns not printed
Class IX	Ornamental designs – Yarn, thread – printed
Class X	Ornamental designs – Woven fabrics – not furniture
Class XI	Ornamental designs – Woven fabrics – furniture, printed patterns
Class XII	Ornamental designs –Woven fabrics – patterns not printed
Class XIII	Ornamental designs –Lace and all other articles

TABLE 2: Month of the Year of Manufacture

C-January	I-July
G-February	R-August
W-March	D-September
H-April	B-October
E-May	K-November
M-June	A-December

TABLE 3: Year of Manufacture-1842-1867

1842-X	1851-P	1860-Z
1843-H	1852-D	1861-R
1844-C	1853-Y	1862-O
1845-A	1854-J	1863-G
1846-I	1855-E	1864-N
1847-F	1856-L	1865-W
1848-U	1857-K	1866-Q
1849-S	1858-B	1867-T
1850-V	1859-M	

TABLE 4: Year of Manufacture-1868-1883

1868-X	1874-U	1879-Y
1869-H	1875-S	1880-J
1870-C	1876-V	1881-E
1871-A	1877-P	1882-L
1872-I	1878-D	1883-K
1873-F		

After 1883, the diamond marks were discontinued and a simpler marking system was instituted, providing only the Rd number and coded year of registration. The numbers simply ascend consecutively from number 1 in 1884. This mark appears on decorative art manufactured in England after 1884.

TABLE 5: Partial Guide to Design Registry Numbers 1884-1945

Year	First Registry Number of Each Year
1884	1
1885	20000
1890	142300
1895	248200
1900	351600
1905	447800
1910	552000
1915	644935
1920	673750
1925	710165
1930	751160
1935	799097
1940	837520
1945	842670

Majolica's Values

The prices found in the captions are in United States dollars. Prices vary immensely based on the location of the market, the venue of the sale, the rarity of the items and/or their glaze treatments, and the enthusiasms of the collecting community. Prices in the Midwest differ from those in the West or East, and those at specialty shows or auctions will differ from those in dealer's shops or through dealer's web pages.

All of these factors make it impossible to create absolutely accurate price listings, but a guide to realistic pricing may be offered. Please note: these values are not provided to set prices in the antiques marketplace, but rather to give the reader a reasonable idea of what one might expect to pay for mint condition majolica pottery. Finding majolica in mint condition is difficult, as this is a soft-bodied earthenware prone to chipping, hairline cracks, and crazing (those fine, spidery-thin cracks in the glaze).

Majolica fish-form teapot and cover with spiny dorsal fin, Minton, c. 1878, of oval form and modeled with seaweed handle and wave-molded base, raised registry and impressed factory marks, 7 1/8" h., 9" l. Note: An identical teapot was sold at Skinner on May 30, 1998 for $28,000 plus buyers premium. *Courtesy of Skinner, Inc. Boston.* $12,000-18,000. Sold at auction for $23,000.

That being said, here are some values for majolica items realized at past auctions. In 2001 at a Sotheby's auction, an example of Minton's majolica teapot fashioned in the shape of a fish with a spiny dorsal fin realized a final price of $35,250, which was nearly three times its high estimated value. This price was achieved even though the lid had cracks, some restoration had taken place, and there were chips on the spout. A rare Minton game pie dish featuring the heads of two mallards and two hares, measuring 18" in length, produced in 1877, sold at auction for $46,750. However, the highest price achieved at that 2001 Sotheby's auction went to a Minton 6" tall figurine of an African man ("Blackamoor") holding a basket of fruit, which sold for $115,750.

Other majolica manufacturers' wares at auction in 2001 also brought considerable sums, although quite a bit lower than the Minton pieces listed. A cheese keeper by George Jones & Sons decorated in a wheat, daisy, and picket fence motif over a turquoise background glaze color sold for $9,350. A figural grape pitcher by T.C. Brown-Westhead, Moore & Company realized $7,150. A triple frog and cattail vase by Copeland sold for $6,050. An Argenta garden seat decorated with a Japanese bird and fan motif, manufactured by Wedgwood, achieved a selling price of $4,125.

In 2000, Minton majolica once again drew top dollar at auction. A Minton rabbit and duck adorned game tureen sold for $60,500. A George Jones & Sons cobalt background cheese keeper decorated with a wheat, daisies, and wooden fence motif reached a top bid of $19,800, while a rare Minton workhorse figure brought $16,500. A figural teapot featuring a three-dimensional cherub rowing a turquoise boat, produced by Holdcroft, sold for $15,400.

Left and above:
Cobalt picket fence and daisy tall size cheese keeper, George Jones, 12" d., 12" h. In 2004, this cheese keeper sold for $10,000.

Friendly Advice

New collectors may enter the majolica market with relatively inexpensive common examples of butter pats, figurines, plates, and pitchers that may be purchased for under $200. For those with limited space, the tiny butter pats (diminutive plates used to provide Victorian diners with individual servings of butter) make an engaging collection. Majolica butter pats were produced in a wide range of decorative motifs and tend to be inexpensively priced.

When looking for novel majolica items, turn to the Continental wares. The French in particular made a wide range of interesting figural wares, including a variety of amusing figural pitchers. American collectors today tend to carry the same bias as American nineteenth century consumers. They gravitate toward the English majolica, overlooking the Continental offerings, hence the Continental pieces are generally more affordable.

Damage significantly affects the value of majolica items. A Minton cat figurine measuring 13.25" on an oval base carried an estimated value of $23,000 for a pristine example. A damaged example of this impressive figurine sold at auction in 2001 for $10,175.

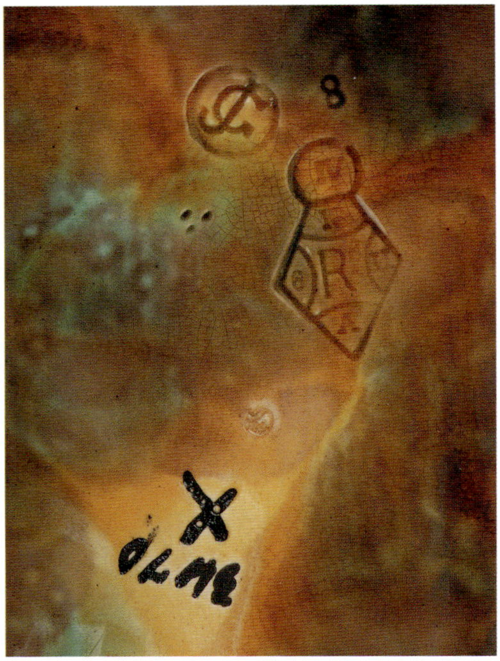

Glaze colors also have an impact on the value of otherwise identical majolica objects. This tray with the cobalt background color sold at auction in 2004 for $3,080. The same tray with a turquoise background sold at the same auction for $4,400. Cobalt butterfly, wheat, and bamboo two-handled tray, George Jones, 13". $3,000-3,300.

Turquoise butterfly, wheat, and bamboo two-handled tray, George Jones, 13". $4,500+.

Glaze colors also have an impact on the value of otherwise identical majolica objects. In 2000, a 13.5" wide George Jones & Sons empty nest game pie dish with twig handles and a cobalt background glaze color sold at auction for $17,600. The same game pie dish with different glaze colors and a turquoise background glaze color sold for $13,200 at the same auction.

Many scarce and rare pieces have risen in value in recent years as they are vied for by an ever growing number of knowledgeable collectors. Whenever diminishing supply meets increasing desire in the world of antiques, modern reproductions are manufactured. Some reproductions are created specifically to fool the unwary. Makers of such fraudulent items attempt to match the glazes, motifs, and manufacturer's marks of rare, original majolica wares as closely as possible. The careful, knowledgeable collector will note that the glazes on such items are less brilliant (the use of majolica's lead glazes, detrimental to the health of the artisans who applied them, ceased early in the twentieth century) and are seldom applied uniformly. The bodies are lighter in weight and slightly smaller in size than the originals. Frequently, the molded decoration is not as sharp as in original majolica wares.

Others reproductions are produced by honest pottery firms in China, Indonesia, Italy, Japan, and Thailand who mark the wares prominently and appropriately with the names of their firms. Such items fill a space in a collection while the original is sought, or when the original is unobtainable. Frequently these honest reproductions are not exact in glaze coloring and do not feature the entirely glazed undersurface of pieces of original Victorian majolica.

Mischief may occur with honest reproductions when they leave the collection of the original owner. Once out of the original collection, disreputable individuals may try to pass off these reproductions as genuine antiques, selling them for much more than they are worth. Make sure you are able to examine all majolica wares closely prior to purchase.

It should be noted that since 1993, Minton & Company has been producing nearly perfect copies of original majolica teapots in celebration of the company's bicentennial. Among the teapots reproduced by Minton & Co. are the Monkey, Blowfish, Cat and Mouse, Chinese Actor, and Monkey and Cockerel. Each reproduction teapot is carefully marked to avoid confusion, including the identification "Fine China" (these are not actual majolica), that teapot's series number, its number in the series released, and the year of production.

Finally, in an article in 2000, Marilyn Karmason alluded to another firm creating reproductions of a wide variety of ceramics, including majolica. This is Mottahedeh & Co., Inc. of New York. Their purpose is quite interesting. The firm provides carefully labeled reproductions of wares displayed in public places such as the White House. Mottahedeh reproductions stand in for the originals in case some souvenir seeker with sticky fingers and little conscience decides to walk away with an item. Better to lose a reproduction than a historical antique. Mottahedeh & Co. produces reproductions for United States Presidents, the State Department, and the Diplomatic Corps. However, you do not have to be a head of state to purchase their reproductions.

Left: Turquoise pointed leaves sardine box with undertray, George Jones. **Below:** Cobalt pointed leaves sardine box and undertray, George Jones. Once again, a difference in background glaze color made a difference in price at auction. The turquoise background sardine box sold for $750 at auction in 2004 while its cobalt background counterpart sold for $700.

Majolica Around the House

The majority of the majolica items displayed in this book are arranged by the rooms in which they would appear in a large Victorian home. While many majolica wares were well within the reach of modest middle class families living in unassuming four room row homes in London or simple shotgun houses in New Orleans, using a sizable, elegant Victorian house complete with a conservatory and smoking-room allows us to separate majolica by its many functions, dealing with each in an appropriate formal or private setting in the home.

House Styles

Technological advancement; improved transportation; the dissemination of architectural designs through increasingly popular pattern books, journals, and the writings of architect Alexander Jackson and landscape gardener Andrew Jackson Downing; the standardization of building materials; a rising middle class; the romanticism of the age; and a fascination with the past combined to create the elaborate, picturesque Victorian homes of the nineteenth century into which majolica fit so well. Balloon framing was instrumental among the technological advancements. Using lightweight wooden framing over a firm foundation and sill, it was possible to create large, complicated, sprawling dwellings unlike anything of any previous age.

Gothic Revival style house in the deep south, possibly in Charleston, South Carolina, or Savannah, Georgia. *Courtesy of the Library of Congress, Prints and Photographs Division, Detroit Publishing Company.*

Andrew Jackson Downing felt the irregular form and roofline, the peaks, towers, and turrets of Gothic Revival architecture were harmonious with the natural world in ways the staid geometries of earlier structures could never achieve. This was well in tune with the public's fascination with the natural world during the nineteenth century. Delicate, intricate decorative gingerbread wood scrollwork for the exterior was now available, cut to order from local carpenters and saw mills. This trim work reflected the original stonework of European Gothic architecture.

Victorian Italianate architecture reflected the forms of the Italian villa. Italianate houses featured towers resembling Italian bell towers, balconies, large porches or verandas, decorative brackets under wide eaves that gave the roof the impression of being nearly flat, and narrow arched or rounded windows.

The Mansard or Second Empire style of the 1870s reflected an appreciation for French architecture. Elaborately constructed chimneys, ornately molded entryways, arched or pointed doorways, and a steeply pitched, curving, nearly flat-topped roof with dormer windows lighting the attic story are all features of Mansard style homes.

However, for Victorian architecture at its most flamboyant, the Queen Anne style beat them all. Fanciful chimneys, turrets, and towers combined to form unusual roof shapes. Projecting bays and stained glass windows added interest while porches and balconies were decorated with all manner of fancy brackets, latticework, and spindles. Here was a house that could handle the most elaborate fantasy concocted by the most impassioned majolica manufacturer.

If none of these styles suited a builder's idea of a picturesque structure, Victorian architects were ready and willing to combine elements from several styles while striving to reach that ideal.

In the United States, by the 1850s, porches were popular across the nation. From the porch one could take in the natural world without leaving home. As the century progressed, porch sizes grew. Front porches became "sitting porches" while additional porches for special purposes developed, including porches for eating, sleeping, and household chores. Majolica appropriate for Victorian conservatories (jardinières, planters, and flowerpots) would have found a place on such porches. Adornments to the porch and yard were considered to be extensions of the interior space and public declarations of the refinement of the home's inhabitants.

Not unlike majolica, the exteriors of Victorian houses were painted in a polychromatic array of colors. Victorians preferred colors that reflected the natural world, including browns, yellows, greens, olives, and gray tones.

Entering the House

It is time to enter the Victorian home, resplendent in all its majolica. A pair of figures of a man and woman, each with basket of flowers, Hugo Lonitz (Haldensleben, Germany, founded 1868, marked their majolica with a two fish in a circle mark), 14" h. $385-425 each.

272

THE CO-OPERATIVE BUILDING PLAN ASSOCIATION, ARCHITECTS, 63 BROADWAY, NEW YORK.

*Shoppell's Modern Houses—*Designs Patented.* *Row of Dwellings, Design No. 268*

PERSPECTIVE.

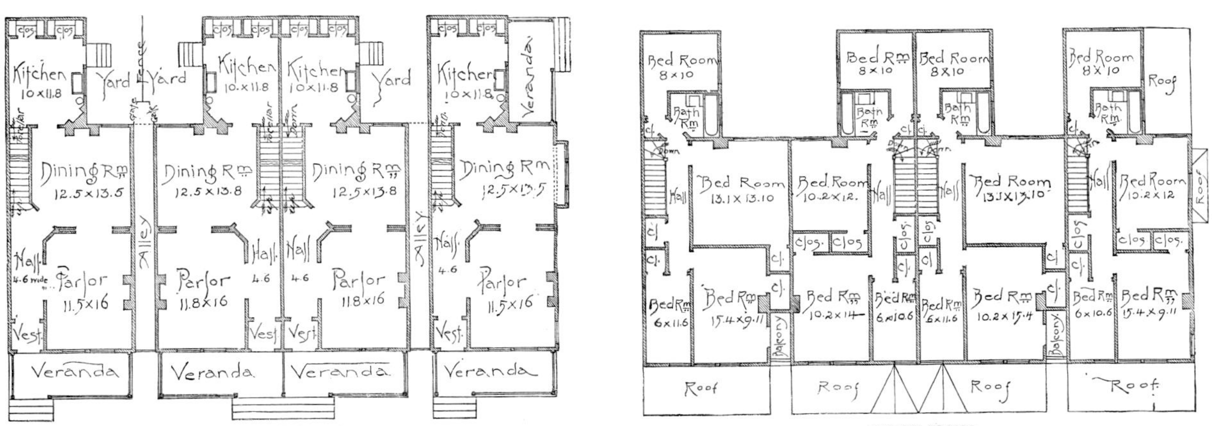

FIRST FLOORS. SECOND FLOORS.

DESCRIPTION.

For explanation of all symbols (* † etc.) see page 42.

GENERAL DIMENSIONS: Extreme width, 76 ft. 6 in.; depth, including verandas, 50 ft. Heights of stories: Cellar, 7 ft.; first story, 10 ft.; second story, 9 ft. 6 in.

EXTERIOR MATERIALS: Foundations, stone; first story, clapboards; second story, clapboards and shingles; roof, tin. Outside blinds to all windows except those of the cellar.

INTERIOR FINISH: Hard white plaster; plaster cornices and centers in halls, parlors and dining rooms. Soft wood flooring and trim. Ash staircase. Chair rail in dining rooms. Bath-rooms and kitchens wainscoted. Interior wood-work finished in hard oil.

COLORS: All clapboards, dark brown. Trim, outside doors, blinds and rain conductors, dark green. Sashes, maroon. Veranda floor, bronze green. Veranda ceiling, light drab. Brick-work, Indian red. Shingles dipped and brush coated reddish stain. Roof painted red.

ACCOMMODATIONS: The principal rooms and their sizes, closets, etc., are shown by the plans. Cellars under all with outside and inside cellar entrance to each house. Two open fireplaces and two mantels for each house, also kitchen range, included in estimate. Sliding doors connect parlors and dining rooms. Bath-rooms with water-closets and bath tubs. Sink and boiler in kitchens. Joint alleyways to rear yards.

COST: $7,820 for four dwellings, † not including heaters. The estimate is based on ‡ New York prices for materials and labor In many sections of the country the cost should be less.

Price for working plans, specifications and * license to build, - - - - - - - - - - - - $25.00

Price for † † bill of materials, - - - - - - 5.00

Address, THE CO-OPERATIVE BUILDING PLAN ASSOCIATION, Architects, 63 Broadway, New York.

FEASIBLE MODIFICATIONS: Heights of stories, colors, sizes of rooms and kinds of materials may be changed. Cellars may be reduced in size or omitted. Fireplaces and mantels, sliding doors, and part or all of plumbing, may be omitted. Verandas may be reduced in size. Gable or mansard roofs may be added, providing an attic or full third story.

Victorian townhouses as they appeared in *Shoppell's Modern Houses* (a pattern book of sorts published by The Co-operative Building Plan Association, Architects of New York in 1890) showing the main floor, three room plan, where many of the less expensive forms of majolica would have been right at home.

The aforementioned shotgun house or modest town house was a three or four room affair with a dining room, parlor, and a bedroom or two. The house explored here is a far grander affair, complete with a variety of specialized public and private rooms.

To easily navigate through the Victorian house, the rooms have been divided under two headings: Private Spaces and Public Places. Private spaces were a family's personal rooms (rooms where guests were not generally received), workrooms, and kitchens. Private spaces listed here include:

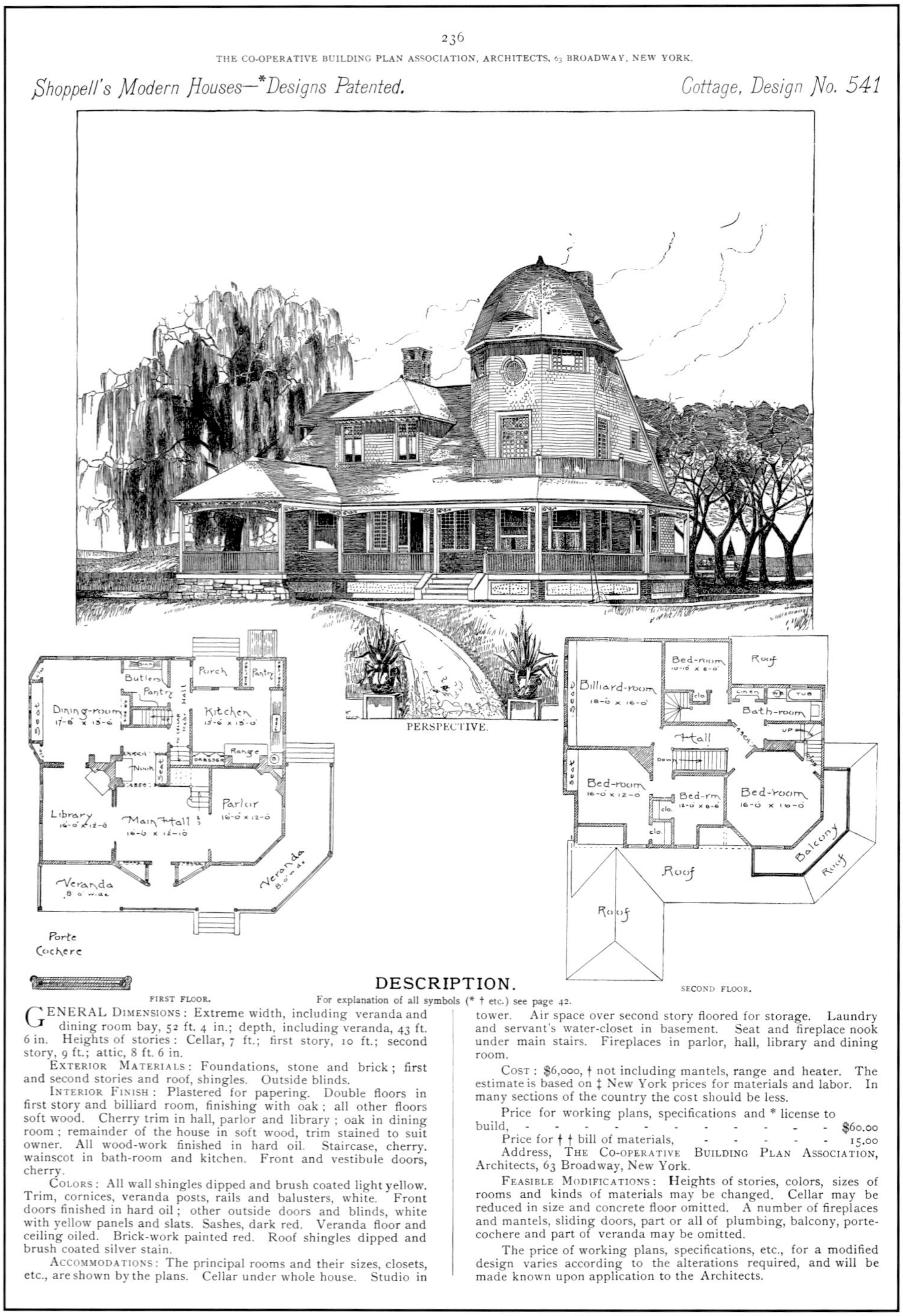

236

THE CO-OPERATIVE BUILDING PLAN ASSOCIATION, ARCHITECTS, 63 BROADWAY, NEW YORK.

*Shoppell's Modern Houses—*Designs Patented.* *Cottage, Design No. 541*

PERSPECTIVE.

FIRST FLOOR. SECOND FLOOR.

DESCRIPTION.

For explanation of all symbols (* † etc.) see page 42.

GENERAL DIMENSIONS: Extreme width, including veranda and dining room bay, 52 ft. 4 in.; depth, including veranda, 43 ft. 6 in. Heights of stories: Cellar, 7 ft.; first story, 10 ft.; second story, 9 ft.; attic, 8 ft. 6 in.

EXTERIOR MATERIALS: Foundations, stone and brick; first and second stories and roof, shingles. Outside blinds.

INTERIOR FINISH: Plastered for papering. Double floors in first story and billiard room, finishing with oak; all other floors soft wood. Cherry trim in hall, parlor and library; oak in dining room; remainder of the house in soft wood, trim stained to suit owner. All wood-work finished in hard oil. Staircase, cherry. wainscot in bath-room and kitchen. Front and vestibule doors, cherry.

COLORS: All wall shingles dipped and brush coated light yellow. Trim, cornices, veranda posts, rails and balusters, white. Front doors finished in hard oil; other outside doors and blinds, white with yellow panels and slats. Sashes, dark red. Veranda floor and ceiling oiled. Brick-work painted red. Roof shingles dipped and brush coated silver stain.

ACCOMMODATIONS: The principal rooms and their sizes, closets, etc., are shown by the plans. Cellar under whole house. Studio in tower. Air space over second story floored for storage. Laundry and servant's water-closet in basement. Seat and fireplace nook under main stairs. Fireplaces in parlor, hall, library and dining room.

COST: \$6,000, † not including mantels, range and heater. The estimate is based on ‡ New York prices for materials and labor. In many sections of the country the cost should be less.

Price for working plans, specifications and * license to build, - - - - - - - - - - - \$60.00

Price for † † bill of materials, - - - - - 15.00

Address, THE CO-OPERATIVE BUILDING PLAN ASSOCIATION, Architects, 63 Broadway, New York.

FEASIBLE MODIFICATIONS: Heights of stories, colors, sizes of rooms and kinds of materials may be changed. Cellar may be reduced in size and concrete floor omitted. A number of fireplaces and mantels, sliding doors, part or all of plumbing, balcony, porte-cochere and part of veranda may be omitted.

The price of working plans, specifications, etc., for a modified design varies according to the alterations required, and will be made known upon application to the Architects.

Victorian house plan from *Shoppell's Modern Houses* for a large cottage with a billiard-room on the second floor.

- Bedrooms: known as "chambers" in wealthy homes; the well-to-do also had "servants' quarters"—bedrooms for the in-house staff.
- Boudoir: where the lady of the house wrote letters and attended to family business.
- Breakfast room/sitting room: well-to-do families took their breakfasts in a separate room from the dining room and this room doubled as a family's informal living room, referred to as a "sitting room."
- Library/study: where the man of the house wrote his correspondence and attended to business.
- Nursery/children's rooms: separate bedrooms for the babies and growing children.
- Workrooms: where family members or servants labored.

The public spaces in a large Victorian house included:

225

THE CO-OPERATIVE BUILDING PLAN ASSOCIATION, ARCHITECTS, 63 BROADWAY, NEW YORK.

*Shoppell's Modern Houses—*Designs Patented.* *Residence, Design No. 650*

PERSPECTIVE.

DESCRIPTION.

For explanation of all symbols (* † etc.) see page 42.

GENERAL DIMENSIONS: Front width, over all, 80 ft. 6 in.; depth including wing, 63 ft. 8 in. Heights of stories: Cellar, 7 ft. 6 in.; first story, 9 ft. 6 in.; second story, 9 ft.

EXTERIOR MATERIALS: Foundations, stone and brick; first story, clapboards; second story, shingles; gables, panels and shingles; roof, shingles.

INTERIOR FINISH: Hard white plaster throughout. Flooring, trim and stairways, all white pine. All interior wood work finished in hard oil.

COLORS: All clapboards, doors, blinds, and gable panels, painted pale yellow. All shingles, stained silver. All trim, white. Brick work cleaned with acid and left natural.

ACCOMMODATIONS: The principal rooms and their sizes, closets, etc., are shown by the plans. There is a cellar, with concrete floor, under the whole house. Two rooms in attic—space for four more. A part of veranda is left uncovered to afford good light for the hall and reception room.

This is a large, comfortable house, imposing in appearance, and of very moderate cost.

COST: $5500, † not including mantels, range and heater. The estimate is based on ‡ New York prices for materials and labor. In many sections of the country the cost should be less.

Price of working plans, specifications and *license to build, - $55.00
Price for †† bill of materials, - 10.00

Address, THE CO-OPERATIVE BUILDING PLAN ASSOCIATION, Architects, 63 Broadway, New York.

FEASIBLE MODIFICATIONS: Heights of stories, exterior materials, interior finish and colors, may be changed. Conservatory, parlor chimney, all fire-places, part of veranda, the covered balcony and the bays, may be omitted. Library and reception room may be connected by doors or they may be made one room. The parlor, library, and reception room may be combined to make one large room.

The price of working plans, specifications, etc. for a modified design varies according to the alterations required, and will be made known upon application to the Architects.

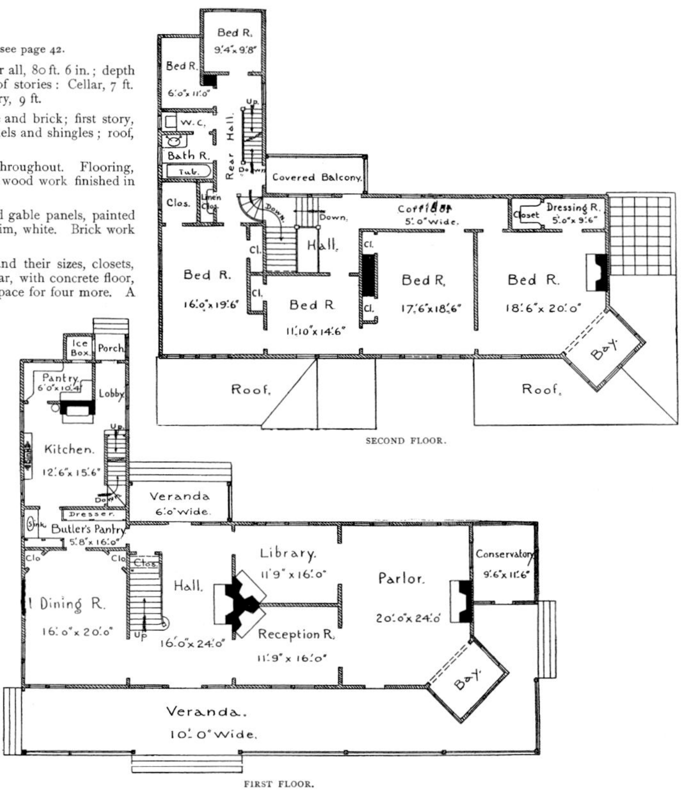

Victorian house plan from *Shoppell's Modern Houses* for a grand home where the most elegant majolica could have been placed in every room. Note the library and conservatory.

- Entryway: the room that ushered guests into the house and set the tone of the home. In a large English Victorian townhouse, the dining room was on the ground floor off the entryway (at street level), the drawing room/parlor was up the staircase on the floor above. Larger, sprawling Victorian homes would have both rooms on the ground floor.
- Billiard-/Smoking-room: a gentleman's domain.
- Conservatory: a greenhouse used to bring nature and warmth into the Victorian home, especially useful and uplifting on a cold winter's day.
- Dining room: where formal Victorian dinners were held, attended by many guests who were served numerous courses.
- Drawing room/parlor: the public room where guests were received, referred to as "salons" in wealthy homes, "parlors" in more modest abodes.

There are a number of Victorian majolica items which could be used in many rooms to add decorative touches or serve useful functions. In this text, however, certain items have been placed in specific rooms, making them much easier to locate. For example, spill vases – which held slivers of wood or paper "spills" used to light fires – were generally useful in every room with a fireplace; however, these decorative majolica spill vases will be found under the heading Public Spaces, and the subheading Drawing Room/Parlor. The majolica tea sets have been placed in the breakfast room for family use as guests would have been served in the drawing room (referred to as the "parlor" by middle class families of lesser means) from a porcelain or silver tea service rather than cheerful earthenware majolica. Inexpensive majolica tea sets may have been used by the household servants in the kitchen rather than the family, for that matter.

Some of the subheadings have been combined for convenience. As the boudoir and library or study served the same function for ladies and their gentlemen, this subheading has been combined. Added to the conservatory are porches and gardens, as ornamental majolica objects were used in both exterior locations as an extension of the interior space and a public statement of both the family's cultural refinement and financial achievement.

The following is a listing of ware types and where they are located in this book.

Locating Majolica By Room

Private Spaces:

Bedroom:
- Box, Glove
- Box, Square
- Candle holders, candlesticks, figural
- Hair-tidy

Boudoir/library/study:
- Fountain pen wipe
- Inkwells

Breakfast room/sitting room:
- Egg holders
- Marmalade pot
- Mugs
- Tea sets & their components: including creamers, sugars, cups & saucers, waste bowls, & tea tiles

Kitchen:
- Bottles, figural
- Pitchers & Toby Jugs
- Syrups

Nursery/children's bedrooms:
- Banks
- Child's tea set
- Figurals, anthropomorphic, cheery

Public Places:

Billiard-/Smoking-room:
- Humidors
- Match boxes, strikers, & holders
- Smoking sets

Conservatory/porch/garden:
- Bud vases
- Cachepots: ornamental pots used to conceal utilitarian flowerpots
- Flower holders
- Garden seats
- Jardinières (with and without pedestals)
- Planters
- Planters, hanging

Dining room:
- Asparagus sets (cradles, servers, plates)
- Bowls
- Butter dishes
- Butter pats
- Cake stands
- Chargers: large circular or oval platter used to serve meat
- Cheese keepers
- Chestnut servers
- Comports
- Condiment servers
- Game dishes & game tureens
- Oyster plates
- Place card holders
- Plates
- Platters
- Punch bowls/sets
- Salts, individual & double
- Sardine boxes
- Sauce dishes
- Servers
- Strawberry servers and components, including plates
- Table centerpieces & center bowls
- Toothpick holders
- Trays
- Tureens
- Wine coolers

Drawing room/parlor:
- Baskets, ornamental
- Chandeliers
- Ewers, ornamental
- Figurals
- Floor urns
- Plaques & trays, ornamental
- Spill vases
- Table lamps
- Vases, mantle and otherwise
- Wall pockets

Entryway:
- Umbrella stands

Private Spaces

Bedroom

Majolica items that were most likely to be found in the Victorian bedroom include boxes, trinket trays, powder boxes, candlesticks, ring stands and trays, match stands, and comb trays. Such items in majolica are rarely found today.

Majolica ewers and basins for washing were also produced. During the early Victorian era, a wash set in every bedroom was a sign of true civility.

Box, Glove

Cobalt bird-footed glove box, Holdcroft, cranes in flight and flowers in relief, brass mounted hinged lid. This beautiful glove box sold at auction in 2004 for $2,000.

Box, Square

Cobalt covered square box with ball and claw feet, Holdcroft, 8.25". The box with matching motif sold at the 2004 auction for $1,400.

Candle holders, candlesticks

Dolphin candle stick, Minton, 8.25" h. $1,500+.

Pair of putti candle holders, George Jones, 12.25" h. $4,000-4,400 pair.

Boudoir/library/study

Hair-tidy

Cat with ball of yarn hair-tidy, J. & T. Bevington (Hanley, Staffordshire, England, 1865-1891), unusual form, 6.25" h. $960-1320.

Fountain pen wipe

Scarce lily fountain pen wipe, Griffen, Smith & Co. $250+.

Inkwells

French figural horse inkwell, very unusual, 10.5" w. $600-800.

Top left: Continental inkwell with cats on bicycles and floral design, 8.5" l. $300-500. **Bottom right:** Continental inkwell with alligator riding bicycle, professional repairs to lid and to rim and feet of base, 8.5" l. $300-500.

Continental figural frog inkwell with glass insert, 3.25" h. $300-500.

Breakfast room/sitting room

Early in the nineteenth century, a breakfast set included twelve cups and saucers with larger teacups than were generally used for other occasions, a sugar bowl, milk pot, teapot, waste bowl, and breakfast plates. Larger sets added a coffee pot, butter boat, and cake plate. By the end of the nineteenth century, fruit and mush had been added to the breakfast menu, each requiring its own plate or bowl.

Having tea at five o'clock in the evening had become a popular Victorian ritual by the 1860s. Tea services for five o'clock tea included the teapot, sugar bowl, creamer, cups and saucers, cup plates, waste bowl, plates, two cake plates, preserve plates, butter plate, a tray, hot-water urn, spoon holder, and at times a syrup or molasses pitcher. If a lady so chose, breakfast and tea could be served on a rotating table in the boudoir.

More formal teas were offered to guests in the drawing room; by 1877 this had become quite the affair, complete with special tea gowns worn by the ladies. On grand country estates, tea was served on the lawn when the weather was right.

Egg holders

Floral double egg cup holder with egg cups, unmarked. $400+.

Marmalade pot

Water lily marmalade pot with attached undertray, unmarked. $105-115.

Mugs

Apple blossom and basket weave mug, George Jones, 5.5" h. $4,000-4,400.

Tea sets & their components: including creamers, sugars, cups & saucers, waste bowls, & tea tiles

Extremely rare cobalt drum shape three-piece tea set with strap and buckle handles, drum stick spout on teapot, George Jones, teapot 6" h. This rare tea set sold at auction in 2004 for $11,000.

Chinaman and coconut figural teapot and matching creamer, Holdcroft, 7" h., 10.5" l. $1,320-1,650.

Extremely rare fish figural teapot with spiny dorsal fins, Minton, 9.5" l., 7" h. In 2004, this rarity sold at auction for $26,000.

Rare dragon handled teapot with birds, flowers, and vine in relief, Royal Worcester (Worcester Royal Porcelain Company, Ltd., Worcester, England, 1862 onward; largely concerned with porcelain production; however, the earthenwares produced were of high quality), 7.5" h. This rare teapot sold at auction in 2004 for $3,000.

Floral three-piece tea set, Victoria Pottery Co. ("VPC", Hanley, Staffordshire, England, 1895-1927). $1,400-1,540 for the set.

Bamboo and fern teapot and undertray, Wardle & Co. (Ltd.) (Hanley, Staffordshire, England, 1871-1910; Wardle Art Pottery Co. Ltd., 1910-1935). (**N**o **P**rice) These two Wardle items sold together at auction in 2004 for $275.

Bamboo and fern teapot, pitcher, and sugar (mismatched lid on sugar), Wardle & Co. NP (**N**o **P**rice) These three Wardle items sold together at auction in 2004 for $275.

Figural cobalt monkey handle teapot, attributed to "J. Roth" (London, England), c. 1880s, 10" l., 7.25" h. This teapot sold at auction in 2004 for $3,630.

Isle of Man three-legged sailor on coil of rope teapot, attributed to William Brownfield & Sons, 9.75". $2,300-2,530.

Cauliflower three-piece tea set, Griffen, Smith & Co. Teapot: $1,350-1,485; sugar: $625+; creamer: $470-525.

Left: Small shell and seaweed coffee pot with straight spout, Griffen, Smith & Co. $1,880-2,070. **Right:** Large shell and seaweed teapot with crooked spout, Griffen, Smith & Co. $1,985-2,085.

Seven piece tea set with teapot, creamer, sugar, and two cups and saucers with floral and dragonfly motif, Clement Massier. $900+ set. This set sold at auction in 2004 for $300.

Bird and fan on pebble ground three-piece tea set, unmarked, possibly Edward Steele (Hanley, Staffordshire, England, 1875-1900). Teapot: $660-725.

Wild rose and rope teapot, unmarked, 7.25". $500+.

Pineapple teapot, unmarked, 6.5" h. $1,055-1,170.

Blackberry teapot, unmarked, 6.5". $400+.

Cobalt teapot with butterfly finial and birds and fans in relief on the side, unmarked, 9.5" l., 5.5" h. $500+.

Rustic floral creamer, George Jones, 3" h. $450+.

Cobalt floral cups and saucers, flower handles on cups, George Jones. $1,100+ for the pair.

Rare figural coconut creamer with chinaman handle, Holdcroft, matches the extremely rare Holdcroft chinaman and coconut teapot, 5" l., 2.5" h. This rarity sold at auction in 2004 for $500.

Honeycomb cup and saucer, Holdcroft. $375+.

Bamboo and fern cup and saucer, Wardle & Co. $375+.

Left:
Cauliflower cup and saucer, Wedgwood. $375+.

Left: Shell and seaweed cup and saucer, Griffen, Smith & Co. $470-520. **Center and right:** Shell and seaweed scalloped edge sauce dishes, Griffen, Smith & Co. $260-285 each. **Front:** Shell and seaweed butter pat, Griffen, Smith & Co. $200+.

Pineapple cup and saucer, unmarked. $375+.

Wild rose and rope cup and saucer, unmarked. $250+.

Cobalt background crane in flight and water lily cups and saucers, unmarked. $375+.

Blackberry and basket weave cup and saucer, unmarked. $250+.

Shell and fishnet waste bowl, S. Fielding & Co., 5.5"d. Waste bowls (a.k.a. slop bowls or slop basins) were included in most tea sets. Dregs from cups of tea were poured into this bowl. These are relatively small capacity bowls that came in several sizes. $650-715.

Left:
Twig and ivy footed tea tile with a portrait in the center, George Jones, unusual form, 7" d. $300+.

Kitchen

The typical middle- and upper-class Victorian house might have as few as two or three servants in the house. These were the cook, housemaid, and parlormaid. If a family had children, a nursemaid was also required. Those households that managed with only two servants employed a cook and a "maid-of-all-work." This household staff was comprised largely of young women in their early twenties who could read and write.

During archaeological investigations at the nineteenth century Laurier House in Ottawa, Canada, once owned by a well-to-do Victorian jeweler and his family, a wide variety of kitchen items were recovered, including baking dishes, pudding and mixing bowls, five teapots, and a majolica pitcher. Many of the wares were plain in design and were believed to be used for either the family's private, informal meals or for the servant's meals. The majolica pitcher recovered was American made. It was made after the mid-1880s and featured a simple tree bark design. This was an inexpensive piece of majolica the archaeologists felt would have been used by the servants themselves. It was believed to be too common to appear on the homeowner's table; but, the bright colors would have been welcomed by the staff, who ate their meals mostly on plain white earthenware featuring a simple embossed wheat pattern—the cheapest tableware available in Canada at that time.

Therefore, while we have pitchers here ranging from the simplest to the wildly extravagant, we will place all of the pitchers in the kitchen for simplicity's sake.

Continental figural pig bottle, unmarked, 6" h. $150-250.

Bottles, figural

Left: Continental cat with fish figural bottle, unmarked, 6.75" h. **Center:** Continental figural pig bottle with red smoking jacket, unmarked, 4.75" h. **Right:** Continental figural vase of dog in red smoking jacket with pipe, unmarked, 6" h. $150-250 each.

Pitchers & Toby Jugs

Cobalt swan topped figural pitcher, J. & T. Bevington, 7.5" h. $960-1,440.

Pink hops and wheat pitcher with lavender ground, Brownfield, 6.5" h. $3,000+.

Hummingbird and bamboo pitcher, S. Fielding & Co., 5.5" h. $500+.

Hummingbird and bamboo pitcher, S. Fielding & Co. (and marked with a registration diamond), 8.5" h. $600+.

Turquoise water lily and iris pitcher, George Jones, 8.25" h. $3,500+.

Turquoise apple blossom and basket pitcher, George Jones, 8" h. $1,800-2,000.

Pink wheat and leaf pitcher with rope rim, George Jones, 7.25" h. $1,800-2,000.

Bamboo pitcher, George Jones, 4.75" h. $500-700+.

Orchid pitcher with leaf handle, George Jones, 7" h. $3,100-3,500.

Pineapple pitcher, George Jones, 7" h. $500-700.

Cobalt pond lily ice lip pitcher, Holdcroft, 9.5" h. $550+.

Figural bear with drum pitcher, Holdcroft, 8.5" h. $1,200-1,500.

Left: Tower jug with jester finial on a hinged pewter lid, Minton, shape no. 1231, 13" h. **Right:** Tower jug with jester finial on a hinged silver lid, Minton, shape no. 1231, 13" h. $1,870+ each. These jugs were used to serve beer.

Left: Pineapple pitcher, Minton, 9.25" h. $800+. **Right:** Pineapple pitcher, Minton, 8" h. $600-800.

Fish on waves pitcher, Shorter & Son (Ltd.) (Stoke, Staffordshire, England, 1905 onward; previously Shorter & Boulton), 5.75" h. $300+.

Cobalt ivy and berry pitcher, Wedgwood, 8" h. $300+.

"Say Please" girl with dog pitcher, unmarked English, 8" h. $400-450.

"Can't You Talk" girl with dog cobalt pitcher, unmarked English, 7" h. $400-450.

Shell and seaweed pitcher, Griffen, Smith & Co., 6.5" h. $845-930.

Left: Shell and seaweed pitcher, Griffen, Smith & Co., 6" h. $845-930. **Right:** Shell and seaweed pitcher, Griffen, Smith & Co., 4" h. $600-800.

Left: Cobalt wild rose pitcher with butterfly spout (listed in the 1884 Griffen, Smith & Co. catalog as the "Rose Jug"), Griffen, Smith & Co., 9.5" h. $600-660. **Right:** Cobalt wild rose pitcher with butterfly spout, Griffen, Smith & Co., 6" h.. $470-520.

Rare full figure Dranem toby jug, by Nimy-les-Mons (Belgium, 1798-1894; in 1894, Nimy joins with Onnaing, forming the Onnaing Society), 13" h. $1,000-1,400. At the turn of the twentieth century, the popularity of the comedian Dranem led to the creation of this jug.

Figural "Pig Waiter" pitcher, La Faïencerie d'Onnaing , 10.5" h. $500-600.

City badger with umbrella, Orchies, 8.5" h. $435-535.

Left: "Jolly Fellow" #3181 face jug, Sarrguemines, 5.5" h. **Center:** "Jolly Fellow" #3181 face jug, Sarrguemines, 6" h. **Right:** "Jolly Fellow" #3181 face jug, Sarrguemines, 5.5" h. $200-330 each, depending on size and scarcity.

Left: Face jug with goatee #3611, Sarreguemines, 8.5" h. $275-375. **Right:** "Jolly Fellow" #3181 face jug, Sarreguemines, 8.5" h. $200-330 each, depending on size and scarcity.

Left:
Double face jug, #2313, Sarreguemines, 8.5" h. $400-475.

Right:
The impressed Sarreguemines mark includes (top to bottom): the name of the firm, the letter code for the decorator on the left under the S in Sarreguemines and the four digit model number to the right, the 227 code for majolica, the last two digits of the year of production (1903 in this case), and the month of production (August in this case).

Left: "The English" #3210 face jug, Sarreguemines, 8" h. **Right:** "The English" face jug glazed in solid green, Sarreguemines with a "Made in Germany" mark and Lorraine crest used while Sarreguemines and Lorraine were in German hands, 8" h. $250-350 each.

Rare face jug with removable lid and matte finish face, Sarreguemines, 9.5" h. $450-550.

"Green hat with pink bow" face jug, #7890, Sarreguemines-type, 8.75" h. $150-450 depending on size and glazing.

"Frowning Face" face jug #8715, Sarreguemines-type, 7" h. $250-450.

"Matelot" ("Sailor" in French) face jug #7892, Sarreguemines-type, 8.5" h. $100-325 depending on size.

Cockatoo decanter, St. Clément, 12" h. $120-330 depending on size and age.

Left: Duck pitcher by St. Clément, 13" h. $165-550 depending on size.
Right: Figural duck pitcher, 12" h. $350-450+.

French cobalt game pitcher, 10.5" h. $350-450.

French figural owl pitcher, 6.75" h. $100+.

Palissy ware jug with oak leaves, acorns and snake wrapped around jug with frog on spout, unattributed, 10" h. $2,000+.

Figural toby pitcher, 9" h. $350-450.

Stork in marsh pitcher with cobalt top and base, unmarked, 9" h. $950-1450+ depending on size.

Bird's nest and begonia leaf pitcher, unmarked, 9.5" h. $495-585.

Bird's nest pitcher, unmarked, 10" h. $495-585.

Cobalt stork in cattails pitcher, unmarked, possibly Eureka, 8.5" h. $550-600.

Cobalt fan and dragonfly pitcher, unmarked, possibly Eureka, 6.25" h. $450+.

Large stork in marsh yellow pitcher with goose head handle, unmarked, 9.75" h. $300-400.

Cobalt fish pitcher, unmarked, 5.75" h. $300-400.

Cobalt wild rose and trellis pitcher, unmarked, 9" h. $300-400.

Cobalt blackberry pitcher, unmarked, 4.5" h. $195-215.

Cobalt wild rose pitcher with yellow top and bottom, unmarked, 6.5" h. $300-400. In a Federal Writers' Project interview in 1938, Mrs. Margaret Weightman told how a majolica pitcher was used in Oswego, Oregon: "That old brown majolica pitcher over there – it holds a gallon – we used to carry down to the men full of milk. And did they lap it up on a hot day!" (Wrenn 1938)

Syrups

Left to right: White sunflower syrup pitcher, Griffen, Smith & Co. $660-770+; Cobalt sunflower underplate, Griffen, Smith & Co., 5" d. $330-360; Cobalt sunflower syrup, Griffen, Smith & Co., lacking thumb lift on lid, $660-770; Cobalt sunflower syrup pitcher, Griffen, Smith & Co. $660-770; Pink sunflower syrup pitcher, Griffen, Smith & Co. $660-770+.

Bamboo motif syrup pitcher, Griffen, Smith & Co. $660-770.

Nursery/children's bedrooms

Banks

Left: Brown dog head figural bank, unmarked. $100-120. Right: Continental face bank, unmarked, 3.75" h. $100-120.

Child's tea set

Nineteen piece children's tea set with teapot, creamer, sugars, plates, cups and saucers, white with floral motif, unmarked. $600-800.

Figurals, anthropomorphic & cheery

Set of three singing frogs, two with song books and one with a mandolin, by Jerome Massier, 3.25" h., 3.75" h., & 4.5" h. $800-880 each.

Continental figural frog floral spill vase, Moehling (Central European pottery firm, early majolica wares were largely smoking sets in solid glaze colors, later wares included refined modeling decorated with polychromatic glazing), 5" h. Spill vases were handy anywhere a fire needed to be lit. Homes began to be fitted with gas lighting in significant numbers in the 1830s. By 1875, homes in most large towns were gas lit. Electric lighting would begin replacing gas lighting in earnest in the last quarter of the nineteenth century. $270-300.

Public Places

Billiard-/Smoking-room

Cigars were symbols of manly status and success for Victorians. After a formal meal, while ladies retired to the drawing room for tea or coffee and conversation, the men drank port and smoked cigars in the dining room … suggesting that humidors and smoking sets were not merely relegated to the billiard- and smoking-room. However, Victorian etiquette declared a gentleman must not smoke in front of a lady. Hence, the smoking-room was a man's territory where he was free to indulge in a cigar without offending the ladies.

A complete smoking set included an ashtray, cigar box, match box, spill case, and tobacco box. Complete sets in majolica are very difficult to find today.

Humidors

Back row: Figural elephant with red smoking jacket humidor, unmarked, 7" h., $715-785; Duck with red cape humidor, unmarked, 5.5" h., $475-525.
Front row: German fox humidor, 4.75" h., $310-340; Continental figural tiger head humidor, 4" h., $310-340.

Back row: Figural pig newlyweds humidor, from Portugal, 8" h. $825+.
Front row: Pig with apron and broom figural humidor, from Portugal, 8" h., $745+; Figural lady duck with bonnet humidor, unmarked, unusual form, 8.75" h., $745+.

Back row: Figural face humidor of man with goatee, unmarked, 5" h. $285-310.
Front row: Figural face humidor of train engineer with cap, unmarked, 6" h., $285-310; Man with green hat humidor, unmarked, 7" h., $375-415; Man with cigar face humidor, unmarked, 5.5" h., $285-310.

Back row: Baby girl with bonnet humidor, unmarked, 5" h., $310-340; Oriental lady humidor, unmarked, 5" h., $310-340.
Front row: Indian maiden face humidor, unmarked, 5.5" h., $285-310. Man with beard and pipe face humidor, unmarked, 6" h., $285-310. Lady with long hair and red headscarf humidor, unmarked, 5" h., $310-340.

Left: Indian head humidor, unmarked, 7". $350-385. **Right:** Large Indian Chief humidor, unmarked, 7.75". $350-385.

Bird and fan motif, turquoise background glaze humidor, unmarked, 5.5" h. $300+.

Match boxes, strikers, & holders

Bird and fan covered match box, Wardle & Co., 4.5" h. $140-155.

Hogarth girl with basket figural match holder, Minton, 7.5" h. $1,450-1,600.

Left: Figural lion match striker (match holder), by B. Bloch & Co. (Bohemia, founded 1871, produced majolica into 1930s), impressed mark "BB #2370". $475-525. **Right:** Continental rabbit and tree stump figural match striker (match holder), by Moehling, 8". $525-575.

Left: Monkey match striker (match holder)/smoke set, marked "HH", 8" w. $350-475. **Right:** Figural match striker (match holder)/smoke set with mouse, melon, flowers and leaves, by B. Bloch & Co., impressed mark "BB", 8". This item sold at auction in 2004 for $550.

Left: Bulldog figural match striker (match holder), unmarked, 5.5" h. $250-275. **Right:** Bulldog figural match striker (match holder), unmarked, 7" h. $275-300.

Top row: Man singing with mandolin match striker (match holder), unmarked, 5" h., $200-220; Figural cowboy with rifle match striker (match holder), unmarked, 10.25" h. $400-440.
Bottom row: Figural owl on log match striker (match holder), unmarked, 4.5" h. $250-275; Indian figural match striker (match holder), unmarked, 8" h. $360-400.

Center: Continental figure with straw hat atop log with baskets match striker (match holder), unmarked, 7" h. $400-440. **Left & right:** A pair of figures, a reclining boy with a slice of melon and a girl, unmarked, 6". $550 pair.

Lady with vases match striker (match holder), unmarked, 8.5" h. $400-440.

Smoking sets

Continental smoke set with checkerboard tray, dice humidor and match holder, two cigarette holders, and a poker chip striker, unmarked, very unusual. $550+.

Conservatory/porch/garden

By the Victorian era, the woodland regions around developed areas were now "tamed," generally free of large carnivores or angry indigenous peoples. Victorians were free to view the relatively safe natural world around them with a romantic eye, rather than as the potential threat to life and limb it had been for their forebears. The Industrial Revolution also provided Victorians with greater access to the world at large than ever before. Explorers returned from around the globe with stories of exotic locales, flora, and fauna. All this led to a fascination with nature. This increasing interest in the natural world was reflected in majolica.

As an expression of this passion for nature, Victorians constructed elaborate gardens, hothouses, and indoor conservatories. Nature, well manicured, was ushered into the Victorian home. To accommodate this trend, potteries produced a wide range of garden accessories, from pedestaled jardinières and garden seats to elaborate planters, flower holders, flowerpots, cachepots, and wall pockets.

Victorians used these flowerpots, planters, and jardinières in and around their homes. Whether found in elegant conservatories or on humble windowsills and exterior staircases, decorative flowers and plants around the house were considered evidence of cultural refinement. If the pots and jardinières were beautiful objects, so much the better.

Flowers were also seen as morally uplifting in the Victorian era. A homemaker might place flowering plants prominently around the home in the hope of elevating the morals of those she lived with. Medicinal herbs were also grown by some in flowerpots and planters, not only for their decorative value, but also for their use in home remedies. Some viewed these medicinal herbs as a sign of God's beneficence, providing natural cures for the children He loved and indirect evidence, through the cessation of pain, of an afterlife in which all pain is banished. When herbal remedies worked, they were perceived as a sign of God's very existence.

Bud vases

Yellow triple hole bud vase with green ribbon and bow, Minton, 6" h. $440+.

Figural flower bud vases, Massier-type, 8" h. $400-440.

Triple hole bud vase of peas in pods, unmarked, 5.5" h. $400-440.

Cachepots: ornamental pots used to conceal utilitarian flowerpots

Cobalt "Asia/Europe" pedestal cachepot/jardinière, Minton, shape no. 1389, date code for 1869, 13.5" h., 12" w. The medallions feature women in profile of different nations, in this case Europe and Asia. Another set features Africa and America. $2,000-3,000+.

Another view of the Cobalt "Asia/Europe" pedestal cachepot/jardinière

Left: Picket fence and floral cachepot with stand, George Jones, 8" h., 8" d. $2,000+. **Right:** Picket fence and floral cachepot with stand, George Jones, 8" h., 8" d. $2,000+.

Bamboo, ribbon, and bow cachepot with undertray, unmarked, 7.5" h., 8" d. $1,100+.

Flower holders

Scarce mottled hedgehog figural flower holder, Wedgwood, 9". This hedgehog sold in 2004 for $600.

Garden seats

Figural garden seat with cobalt pillow seat supported by small Blackamoor figure among cattails on a rock base, Holdcroft. $4,000-6,000.

Turquoise ground garden seat, George Jones, c. 1874, birds, dragonflies, pond lilies, and cattails in colored relief, wicker modeled top and foot rim, impressed registry and factory mark, printed pad mark, 18" h. *Courtesy of Skinner, Inc. Boston.* $4,000-6,000. Sold at auction for $5,175.

Cobalt stork and bamboo garden seat, attributed to Forester, 21" h. $3,000-5,000.

Jardinières (with & without pedestals)

Monumental floor jardinière with large vine handles and rim of grape clusters, by Copeland, cobalt ground with faces of mythological figures in high relief. This massive jardinière sold in 2004 at auction for $3,350.

Turquoise calla lily jardinière, George Jones, 12" d., 10.75" h. $3,780-4,150.

Cobalt water lily and fly jardinière with bamboo base, George Jones, 10" w., 8.5" h. $3,400-3,740.

Crate and insect footed jardinière, George Jones, unusual form, 7.75" h., 7" w. $2,000-4,000. With damage, including an old Victorian staple repair and a rim chip, this piece sold for only $125 at auction in 2004.

Cobalt footed jardinière with ladies head handles and garland drapes, Holdcroft, 11" w., 7" h. $2,350-2,585.

Pond lily oval window jardinière, Holdcroft, a very unusual footed form, 17" l., 6.5" h. $2,000-4,000.

Turquoise floral jardinière and undertray, Holdcroft, cobalt accents, 9" h., 9" d. $2,000+.

Majolica jardinière, Minton, c. 1880, oval form with lobed body and scrolled handle, foliate and floral relief to a stippled ground, unmarked, large, 19". *Courtesy of Skinner, Inc. Boston.* $2,000-4,000. Sold at auction for $4,600.

Ram's head jardinière, Minton, 14.75" h., 19.5" w. $2,000-4,000.

Large wishing well jardinière, by Choisy-Le-Roi (France, produced majolica from the 1860s to 1910), measuring 27" h. sitting atop a tree trunk pedestal base by Massier, measuring 26" h. Combined, these items measure 58" overall. This eye-catching combination sold at auction in 2004 for $1,000.

Palissy shells, fern, and leaf jardinière, Thomas-Victor Sergent (Paris, France, c. 1870-1880), 7.5" h., 10" d. $1,000-1,200.

Large French birds on branch, blackberry, floral, and leaves oval jardinière, 15" w., 8" h. $700+.

Planters

Small dolphin footed planter with griffins on ends, Hugo Lonitz, cobalt accents, 6" w., 5" h. $500+.

Small figural swan planter, Delphin Massier, 6" l., 3.25" h. $500-700.

Figural bird planter, Jerome Massier, 11" w., 7" h. $300+.

Continental figural planter, a man with a tambourine in front of bamboo pipes, 8.5" h. $300+.

Planters, hanging

Cobalt griffin head hanging planter with leaves and foliage in high relief, Sarreguemines, shape no. 557, 11" d., 6" h. $770-850.

Dining room

Display was an important aspect of any formal Victorian dinner. The affair was designed to impress one's guests and raise one's social, and possibly business, standing in the community. Impressive majolica tablewares and centerpieces helped provide the proper impact. During the course of a formal dinner, majolica wares would be used to serve a variety of courses. Any serving pieces that did not receive heavy use from a knife and fork were produced in majolica. For a formal dinner for twelve, ten courses could be served prior to dessert, coffee, and walnuts.

Fruit and oysters in abundance were impressive on the Victorian table. New national railway systems and refrigerator cars allowed what had once been exotic and seldom eaten delicacies to grace nineteenth century tables. Fruit was eaten with special knives and forks, never with the hands. Strawberries received their own special server, complete with sugar and cream containers. Strawberries were also served with afternoon teas. Oysters were favorites of every social class. However, an ostentatious display of oysters at a party using special majolica oyster servers and plates surely raised one's status in the eyes of guests.

Major majolica serving pieces came and went from the table with each course. The impact these items made on the guests was fleeting. However, impressive centerpieces and small majolica wares remained and reinforced a positive lasting impression. These small pieces included butter pats and individual salts.

Dessert services were designed to finish the impressive formal dinner with style. The service itself, lavishly decorated with tasteful flowers and fruit, consisted of low and high comports, at least two cake plates, and twelve dessert plates.

Asparagus sets (cradles, servers, plates)

Asparagus server with attached undertray, Minton, shape no. 1549, date code for 1874, 10" l. $1,500+.

Two asparagus trays and cradles, by Longchamp (Digion, France, recognized for their majolica asparagus servers, oyster plates, and wall pockets), 13.5" l. $650+ each.

Asparagus plate, Longchamp, 10" d. $200-300.

Eight piece asparagus set with four plates, sauce boat, platter, and platter with cradle, by Longchamp. This set sold at auction in 2004 for $900.

French three-piece asparagus covered barrel with undertray, unmarked, possibly Keller and Guerin, tray 14" l., barrel 11" l., 7.5" h. $1,650-2,200.

Unusual cobalt French wagon asparagus cradle and matching undertray, 11" l. $500+.

French asparagus cradle with attached undertray, 11" l. $350-450.

A French asparagus plate, 10" d. $200-300.

Left: French asparagus plate, 9.5" d. $200-300. **Right:** French asparagus plate, 9" d. $200-300.

Bowls

Cobalt shell bowl with three shell feet, Holdcroft, 9.5" d. $500-550.

Oak leaf oval bowl with pink center, Griffen, Smith & Co., 12.5" d. This bowl sold at auction in 2004 for $500.

Shell and seaweed bowl, Griffen, Smith & Co., 8.5" d. $375-415.

Mottled leaf and floral shrimp dish with shrimp finial, unmarked, 6.75" d., 4.75" h. $250-275.

Butter dishes

Three-piece butter dish with shrimp finial atop a bed of leaves, ferns, and flowers, by Samuel Alcock & Co. (Cobridge, Burslem, Staffordshire, England, 1826-1859), 6.5" d. $500-600.

Bird and fan covered butter dish, Wardle & Co., 8.5" d. $450+.

Cauliflower covered butter tub, Sarreguemines. $300+.

Blackberry and tree bark covered butter tub with attached tray and insert, unmarked, 6.5" d. across the attached base. $300+.

Shell and waves covered butter dish with insert, unmarked. $300+.

Butter pats

Four pansy butter pats by Copeland. $250+ each.

Left: Two fan and insect butter pats, with light green ground or white ground, by S. Fielding & Co. $250+ each. **Center:** Fan-shaped butter pat with pink ground, by Eureka Pottery, $295-325. **Right front:** Morning glory on napkin butter pat with handle, unmarked. $165-180. **Right back:** Morning glory on napkin butter pat. $125-140.

Left: Rare fish-shaped butter pat, unmarked, 4.75" l. This rare item sold at auction in 2004 for $400. **Center:** Shell and seaweed butter pat, unmarked. $135-150. **Right:** Rare butter pat with Oriental ship and fan motif, by S. Fielding & Co. $325-360.

Top, left to right: Pond lily butter pat, Griffen, Smith & Co. $190-210; Multi-color pansy butter pat, Griffen, Smith & Co. $160-175; Green pond lily butter pat, Griffen, Smith & Co. $165-185.
Bottom: Three geranium butter pats, Griffen, Smith & Co. $160-175 each.

Five begonia leaf on basket butter pats, Griffen, Smith & Co., considered rare. $310-340 each.

Set of four maple leaf on plate butter pats, Griffen, Smith & Co. $160-175 each.

Top row, left to right: Mottled leaf butter pat, unmarked. $125-140; Mottled leaf butter pat, unmarked. $125-140; Mottled pink, green, yellow, and brown butter pat, unmarked. $125-140.
Bottom: Maple leaf on basket butter pat, unmarked. $125-140.

Cake stands

Tall dolphin footed cake stand with scenic center, Wedgwood, 9" d., 5" h. $750+.

Pond lily and stork tall cake stand, unmarked, 9.5" h., 10.5" d. $550+.

Chargers: large circular or oval platter used to serve meat

Floral charger, Minton, 14" d. $2,200+.

Cheese keepers

Rare cobalt ground cheese keeper with a cow on one side and a bull on the other among apple trees with an apple finial, attributed to Forester, 11" h. $3,500+.

Opposite page, top:
Left: Dogwood and Woven Fence motif, turquoise ground, full-sized cheese keeper, George Jones, 12.5" h. $5,000+.
Right: Dogwood and Woven Fence motif, turquoise ground, cheese keeper, George Jones, 10" h. $5,000+.

Opposite page, bottom:
Turquoise daisy floral cheese keeper, George Jones, 10.5" d., 7.5" h. This cheese keeper sold at auction in 2004 for $3,500.

Pink ground rope and fern paneled cheese keeper, unmarked, 11" d., 10" h. $1,800+.

Picket fence and floral cheese keeper, full-sized, George Jones, 11" h. $3,550+.

Cobalt ground bird on branch and water lily cheese keeper, unmarked, 7" h. $1,600+.

Bird on branch cheese keeper with ribbon and bow accents, unmarked, 7" h. $1,600+.

Wedge-shaped orchid cheese keeper, unmarked, 12" l., 8" h. $900+.

Mottled wedge cheese keeper, 9.75" l., 6" h. $500+.

Chestnut servers

Chestnut server, Minton, shape no. 594, date code for 1873, 9.5" d. $2,000-2,200.

Comports

Turquoise shell comport, George Jones, 9" d., 5" h. $700-1,000.

Two chestnut leaf on napkin low comports, George Jones, 9.25" d. $600-800 each.

Pond lily comport with water lily, cattail, and lily pad base, George Jones, 9.5" d., 5.5" h. $700-1,000.

Pond lily low comport, Holdcroft, 8.75" d. $465+.

Cobalt ground leaf comport, Holdcroft, 9.25" d. $465+.

Mottled shell comport with shells and seaweed on base, Holdcroft, 9.5" d., 7" h. $860-950.

Back row: Pair of triple dolphin and shell comports, Wedgwood, 9"d, 7"h. $675-750 each. **Front row:** Mottled shell plate on three dolphin feet, Wedgwood, 9" d. $300-500.

Classical style lion footed comports with water lily and dragonfly reticulated tops, Wedgwood, 9" d., 5.5" h. $675-750 each.

Argenta strawberry comport, Wedgwood, 8.5" d. $250-300.

Large French figural comport with mermen and seahorses supporting bowl with griffin faces, attributed to Thomas-Victor Sergent, 15.5" h. $1,400+.

Condiment servers

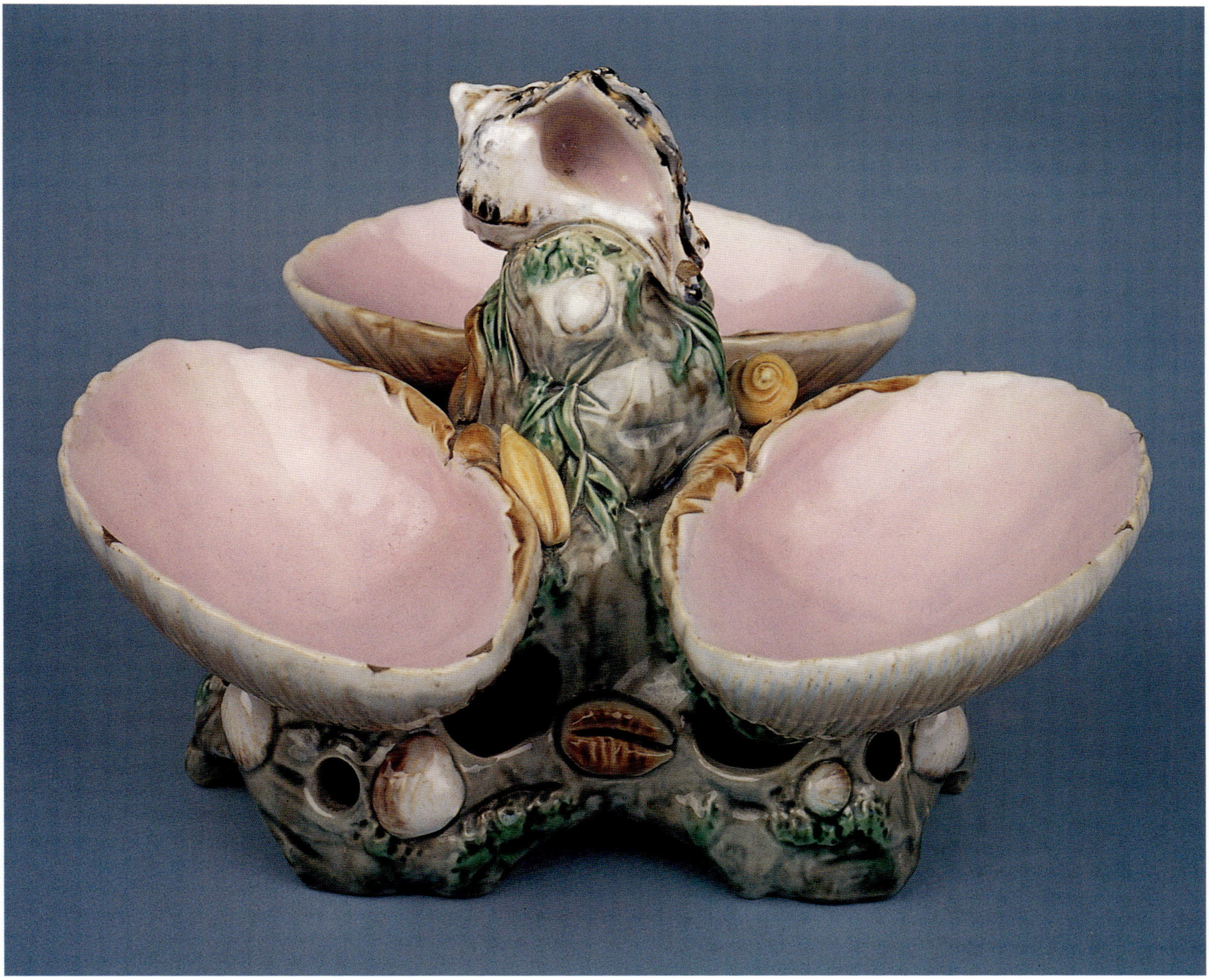

This is a rare form: a triple shell seafood condiment server with shell handle by Minton, shape no. 1557, date code for 1870, 5.5" h., 8" w. In 2004, this rare server sold at auction for $2,530.

Game dishes & game tureens

Front left: Quail game pie dish with quail on lid with bed of wheat, pointed leaf and wheat base, George Jones, 11" l. $3,300+. **Back right:** Quail game pie dish, George Jones, 11.75"l. $3,300+.

Basket weave game pie dish with mallard ducks on a bed of ferns on the cover, and with an insert, Victoria Pottery Co., 12" l. $1,200+.

Boar's head game tureen with brown ground trimmed in green, insert included, Victoria Pottery Co., 12" l. $600-800.

Love birds game pie dish with winged griffin handles, flowers, leaves, game, ribbon, and bows in relief, Wedgwood, 10" l. $1,200+.

Lavender covered game tureen with liner, 9" l. $800-1,000.

Oyster plates

Small turquoise six well oyster plate with raised center shell, George Jones, 8" d. $3,500-3850.

Left: Turquoise ground six well oyster plate with green center, Minton, shape no. 1323, 9" d. $550-850+. **Right:** Pink ground six well oyster plate, Minton, shape no. 1323, date code for 1874, 9" d. $685-750.

Fish and seaweed oyster plate, Minton, shape no. 2366, 11" d. $660-725.

St. Louis pattern oyster plate with cobalt and turquoise wells, Wedgwood, 9" d. $3,500-3,850.

Left:
Ocean, shells and seaweed oyster plate with alternating lavender and white wells, Wedgwood, 9" d. $2,100+.

Place card holders

Six floral place card holders, Delphin Massier, 3.5" h. In 2004, at auction these six place card holders sold for $2,700. One French butterfly and floral figural place card holder, 3.25" h. $500+.

Plates

Basket weave and bamboo dessert plate with mottled center, George Jones, 9.25" d. $350-385.

Chestnut leaf on napkin dessert plate, George Jones, 9" d. $350-385.

Pineapple plate, George Jones, part of a dessert set from c. 1870, 9" d. $545-600.

Leaf and ferns dessert plate with turquoise ground, George Jones, 8.5" d. $350-385.

Picket fence plate with mottled center, George Jones, 8" d. $350-385.

Yellow dogwood plate (scarce to find in yellow ground glaze color), Holdcroft, 8.5" d. This plate sold at auction in 2004 for $750.

Cobalt ground leaf plate, Holdcroft, 8.25" d. $400-600.

Triple fish and fern plate, Wedgwood, 9" d. $565-625.

Left: Cobalt and turquoise fan and floral plate, Wedgwood, 6.5" d. $200-300. **Right:** St. Louis pattern, Oriental floral plate, Wedgwood, 6.25" d. $400-600.

Cobalt lobster plate, Wedgwood, 8.5" d. $1,000+.

Cobalt monkey on branch plate, Wedgwood, 8.5" d. $1,000+.

Yellow grape and leaf plate, Wedgwood, 9" d. $565-625.

Ocean plate, Wedgwood, 9" d. $330-365.

Fans plate, Wedgwood, 9" d. $550-600.

Floral plate with reticulated border, Wedgwood, 9" d. $500-550.

Chrysanthemum plate, Wedgwood, 9" d. $450+.

Left: Bird and fan Argenta plate, Wedgwood, 9" d. $375-415.
Right: Bird and fan Argenta plate, Wedgwood, 8.25" d. $350-375.

Two Argenta Oriental pattern floral plates, Wedgwood, 8.25" d. $280-310 each.

Plate featuring mottled tortoise shell glaze center with a basket weave edge, Wedgwood, 9" d. $240-265.

Maple leaves on pink ground plate, Griffen, Smith & Co., 9" d. $620-685.

Left to right: Cauliflower plate, Griffen, Smith & Co., 9" d. $375-425; Cauliflower plate, Griffen, Smith & Co., 8" d. $375-425; Cauliflower saucer, Griffen, Smith & Co. $125+.

Left to right: Maple leaf on brown glazed basket plate, Griffen, Smith & Co., 8.5" d. $375-425; Maple leaf on pink glazed basket plate, Griffen, Smith & Co., 9" d. $375-425.

Left to right: Maple leaf on pink glazed basket plate, Griffen, Smith & Co., 8" d. $375-425; Maple leaf on yellow glazed basket plate, Griffen, Smith & Co., 8" d. $375-425.

Pond lily plate, unmarked, 9.75" d. $140-155.

Platters

A Minton platter patterned after Palissy's early Greco-Roman classically styled work, 15" l. $1,540+.

Fan and insect with scroll platter with turquoise pebble ground, S. Fielding & Co., 13" l. $350-385.

Platter with lady and serpent in the sea, Wedgwood, 15" d. $750+.

Cobalt ground with sickles and wheat harvest platter, Wedgwood, 13" d. $650+.

Argenta sunflower and begonia leaf platter, Wedgwood, 11" l. $300+.

Argenta Ocean platter, Wedgwood, dated by the impressed code accompanying Wedgwood manufacturer's mark to May 1880. $600+.

Argenta corn and poppy platter, Wedgwood, 13" l. $500+.

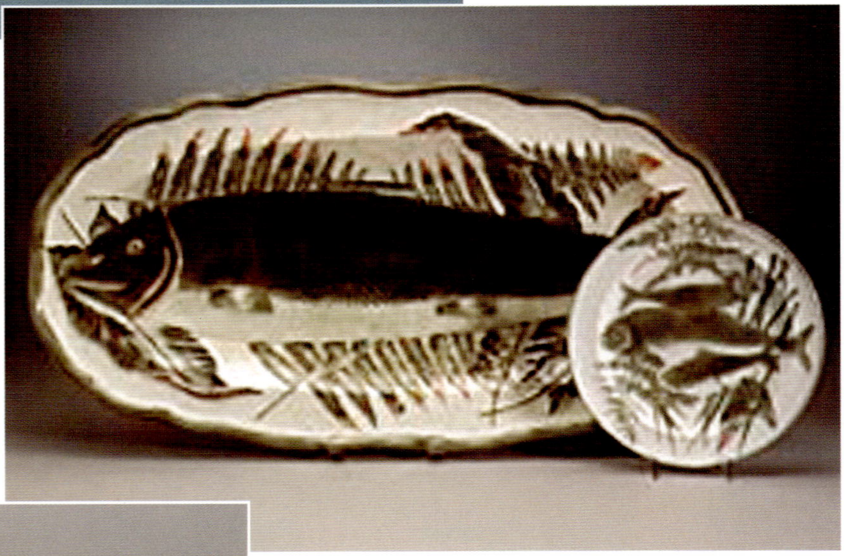

Twenty-two piece Argenta Ware fish service, Wedgwood, c. 1880, each with molded fish and foliage, including twenty plates, 8.75" d.; and two oval platters, 24.75" l., 25.25" l., impressed marks. *Courtesy of Skinner, Inc. Boston.* $1,600-2,400. Sold at auction in 2003 for $5,750.

Dragonfly platter, an unmarked American example, c. 1884, 11.5" l. $565-625.

Corn platter, unmarked, 13" l. $380-425.

Geranium platter with lavender flowers, unmarked, 12" l. $600+.

"Eat Thy Bread With Thankfulness" platter with fish on begonia leaf, unmarked, 12.75" l. $565-625.

Pear and leaf platter, unmarked, 13" l. $565-625.

Punch bowls/sets

Rare grape and vine punch set with a punch bowl and eight matching cups, Wedgwood, the punch bowl measuring 10.5" d. x 6.5" h. $2,500+.

Salts, individual & double

Pair of lily individual salts, Griffen, Smith & Co. $250-275 each.

A pair of French hen and rooster figural double salts, 3.5" h. $250+ each.

Figural chicken double salt, Thomas-Victor Sergent, unusual form, 4" w. $375-415+.

Sardine boxes

Cobalt ground sardine box with attached undertray, Holdcroft. $1,700+.

Argenta Oriental floral sardine box, Wedgwood. $950+.

Yellow sardine box with attached undertray, unmarked. $1,500-1,700.

Cobalt sardine box with attached undertray, fish on bed of seaweed on cover, unmarked. $1,500-1,700.

Brown sardine box with attached undertray and overlapping fish on lid, unmarked. $1,500-1,700.

Sauce dishes

Ribbon and bow sauce dish, Wedgwood, 7" d. $300+.

Servers

Cobalt ground basket weave and leaves two part server with twig handle, George Jones, 13" w. $625+.

Strawberry servers & components, including plates

Bird on floral tray strawberry server with cream and sugar, George Jones, 11" w. $2,795-3,000.

Strawberry server with cream and sugar, George Jones, 14.5" w. $2,360-2,600.

Turquoise strawberry creamer, George Jones, 3.5". In 2004, this creamer sold alone at auction for $325.

Left: Strawberry spoon with pierced bowl, George Jones. In 2004, this spoon sold for $525 at auction. **Right:** Strawberry ladle, George Jones, 4.25" l. In 2004, this ladle sold at auction for $600.

Left: Turquoise strawberry server with twig handles, Holdcroft, 11.5" l. $800-1,200. **Right:** Cobalt rustic floral strawberry basket with twig handles, Holdcroft, 12" l. $800-1,200.

Two individual strawberry plates, Minton, 8.5" l. $750-850 each.

Table centerpieces & center bowls

Table center with putti riding dolphin atop shell and coral base while holding shell, George Jones, 15" h., 13.5" w. $5,000+.

Water lily and basket weave round table center flower holder, George Jones, 15" d., 2" h. $6,000-8,000.

Rabbits under cabbage table center, Minton, shape no. 1451, date code for 1873, 9.5" l., 4.5" h. $9,000-10,000.

Argenta angel and putti center bowl and tray, Wedgwood. $2,800+.

Figural center bowl, Hugo Lonitz, 11" l., 8" h. $800-1,200.

French triple swan table center, 16.25" d., 8" h. $500+.

Toothpick holders

Left: Cobalt deer and trees toothpick holder, Wilhelm Schiller & Sons (W.S. & S.), 2" h. $225-250. **Right:** Moth and butterfly toothpick holder, unmarked, 1.75". $225-250.

Continental chicken with barrel figural toothpick holder, unmarked, 4.75" h. $225-250.

Trays

Chestnut leaf tray with mottled center, George Jones, 12" d. $800+.

Cobalt basket weave tray with yellow rope border and green floral center, George Jones, 10.25" d. $700-800.

Turquoise leaf tray with twig handle, lacking bird or squirrel, George Jones, 10.25" w. $800-1,000.

Dark green pond lily round tray/ underplate, Minton, 14" d. $400-500.

Very rare cucumber tray, Minton, date code for 1871, shape no. 1572, 15" l. $1,320-1,760+.

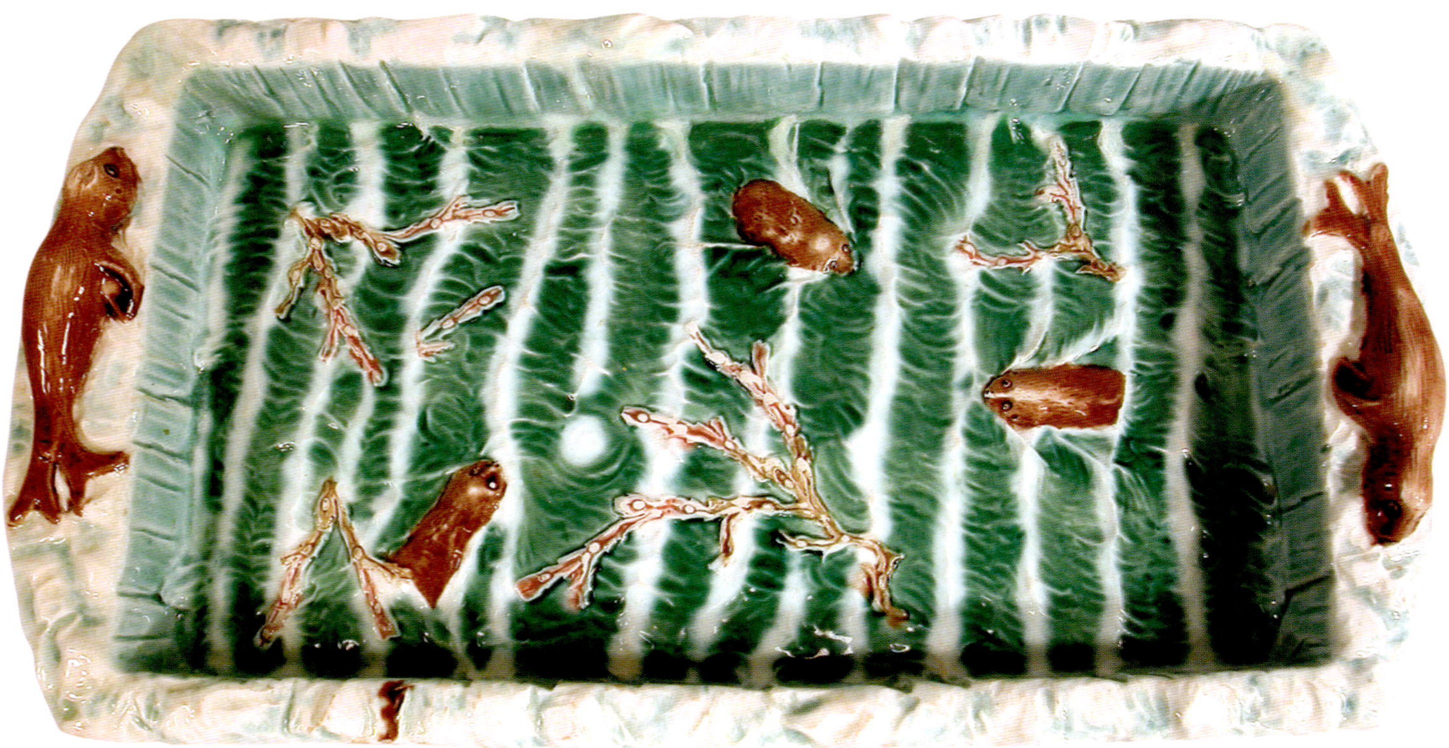

Fanciful seal tray with seal handles and seals swimming in the base among seaweed, Wedgwood, 16.75" l. $800+.

Heart-shaped vegetable tray, Wedgwood, unusual form, 7" l. $300-330.

Cobalt ground shell-shaped tray with tortoiseshell glazed center, Wedgwood, 12" l. $300-330.

Dark green leaf and wicker handled tray, Wedgwood, 9.5" l. $300-330.

Turquoise ground basket weave grape tray with twig handles, Wedgwood, 9.5" d. $600-660.

Three oak leaf trays, one with a yellow border and two with pink, Griffen, Smith & Co., 12" l. $625-690 each.

Three grape trays, two with pink background glaze and one with white, Griffen, Smith & Co., 10" l. $625-690 each.

Tureens

Tureen with bull, horse, and calf head handles, with undertray, Brownfield, 9" w. This tureen sold at auction in 2004 for $1,000.

Boar's head covered tureen with floral, leaf, and vine motif on base, Victoria Pottery Co., 15" l. $600-800.

Covered tureen with grapes and vine in high relief on base and cauliflower finial on cover, with insert, Wedgwood, 7.5" l. $900-990.

Argenta Oriental floral round covered tureen, Wedgwood, 10" d. $1,200+.

Covered strawberry tureen, Sarreguemines. $465-500.

French barn-shaped covered tureen with chicken handles and hen with chicks on cover, unusual form, 8" l., 7" h. $1,000-1,400.

Wine coolers

Opposite page and below:
Turquoise wine cooler with griffin mask and snake handles, Minton, shape no. 946, date code for 1871, 8.5" h., 7.5" d. $7,500+.

Drawing room/parlor

In the drawing room, elegant majolica objects could be found on the fireplace mantle, in the whatnot case, on top of built in bookshelves, in recessed alcoves, on tabletops, and hanging from the ceiling. Heavy drapes were employed in the drawing room to protect the carpets found there. Carpets and wallpaper became increasingly common in the homes of the affluent and rising middle class as the nineteenth century progressed. Brightly glazed majolica wares would stand out nicely in these ornate, dimly lit confines.

Baskets, ornamental

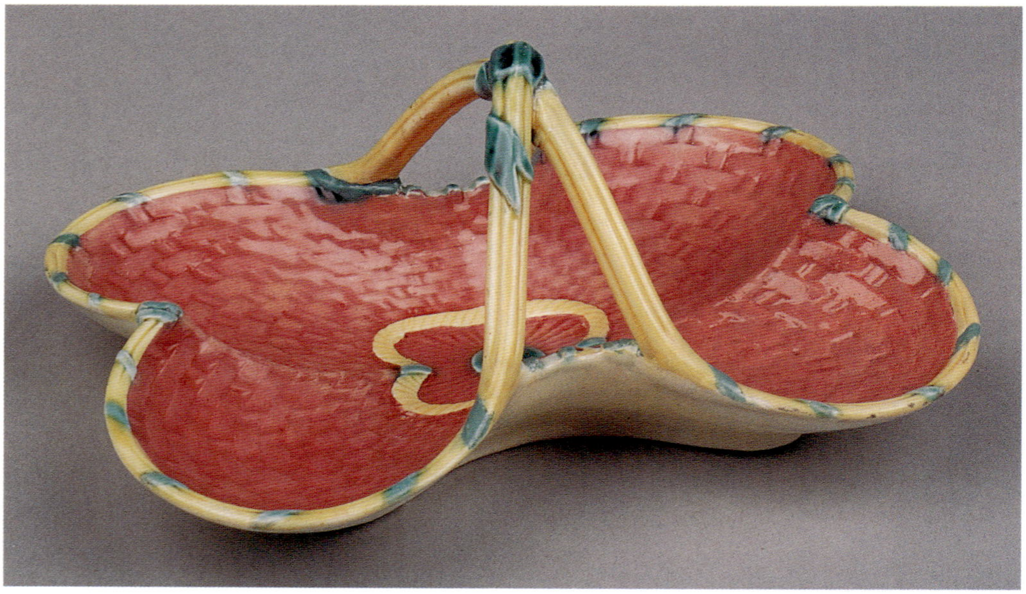

Pink background basket weave basket with yellow rim and handle wrapped with green ribbon, Wedgwood, 8" l. $500+.

Rare begonia leaf and wicker baskets, Griffen, Smith & Co., 12" l. $800+ each.

Chandeliers

This is an extremely rare turquoise ground Neo-Classical hanging chandelier. The vase and bottom plate/bowl of the chandelier were manufactured of majolica by George Jones & Sons. Each majolica section is adorned with three ladies connected with pink ribbons and bows, grapes, vines, and foliage. Majolica is attached to a cast brass five light fixture with decorative rings, originally designed to use gas and later converted to electricity; this item appears to be an original factory made fixture. The vase portion measures 14" h.; the majolica plate/bowl measures 12" d. The chandelier overall measures 30" w. x 28" h. $10,000+.

Ewers, ornamental

Ewer with puttis, leaves, and flowers in high relief and a single putto clinging to the twig handle, Brownfield, 16.5" h. $1,500+.

Cobalt ewer with swan atop cattails, Hugo Lonitz, 15" h. This ewer sold at auction in 2004 for $1,200.

Figurals

Parrot on stump figure, Minton, 12.5". $950-1,045.

Pedestal with figures of three hunters with dog and game, Minton, shape no. 657, date code for 1866, 8.5" $950-1,045.

Majolica "Model of a Bull," Wedgwood, c. 1878, mottled glazes to the body, mounted on a raised and cut-corner rectangular base, impressed mark, 11.75" h., 17.75" l. *Courtesy of Skinner, Inc. Boston.* $2,000-4,000. Sold at auction for $9,200.

Partridges with cattails under oak tree with oak leaves and acorns stand, Hugo Lonitz, 13.25" h. This figure sold at auction in 2004 for $4,620.

Continental cats under tree figure, 5.75" h. $120-140.

Pair of figures, lady with baskets of flowers and umbrella, man with suitcase, umbrella, and top hat, unmarked, 14" h. $350-385 each.

Figural of boy on pillow balancing covered egg with feet, unmarked, 8.5" h. $120-140.

Floor urns

Cobalt Classical two piece floor urn, George Jones, 18" h. $3,000-5,000.

Plaques & trays, ornamental

French Palissy ware lobster plaque, cobalt ground, 15.5" l. $2,500-3,500+.

Lobster tray, Longchamp, 14.5" l. $2,500-3,500+.

Shelves

A pair of wall bracket shelves, each featuring a putto (a boy or a girl) among leaves, Thomas-Victor Sergent, 9.5" h., 7.5" w. It is interesting to note that there is no glaze on the top surface of the shelf. $1,400-1,600+ pair.

Spill vases

Left: Vintager boy with basket, spill vase, Minton, 7.5" h. $1,500+. **Right:** Boy vintager with basket, spill vase, Minton, 8" h. $1,500+.

Figural owl spill vase with large owl on tree stump and small owl on fence, unmarked, 10" h. $500-700.

Table lamps

Large triple stork and cattail table lamp, 11.5" h. $800-1,000.

Vases, mantle and otherwise

Opposite page:
Pheasant and rabbit figural vase, Brownfield, 14" h. While the estimated value for this vase has been around $1,260-1,385, it sold for $5,500 at auction in 2004.

Ivy and berry two-handled vase, Brownfield, 6.75" h. $300-330.

Pair of impressive mantle vases with cobalt ground and floral and leaf motif, Copeland, 11.5" h. $4,000-6,000 pair.

Cobalt and turquoise lily vase, Minton, shape no. 293, 6.5" h. $500+.

Vase with basket weave and applied floral motif, Minton, shape no. 1287, date code for 1870, 6.75" h. $1,000-1,400.

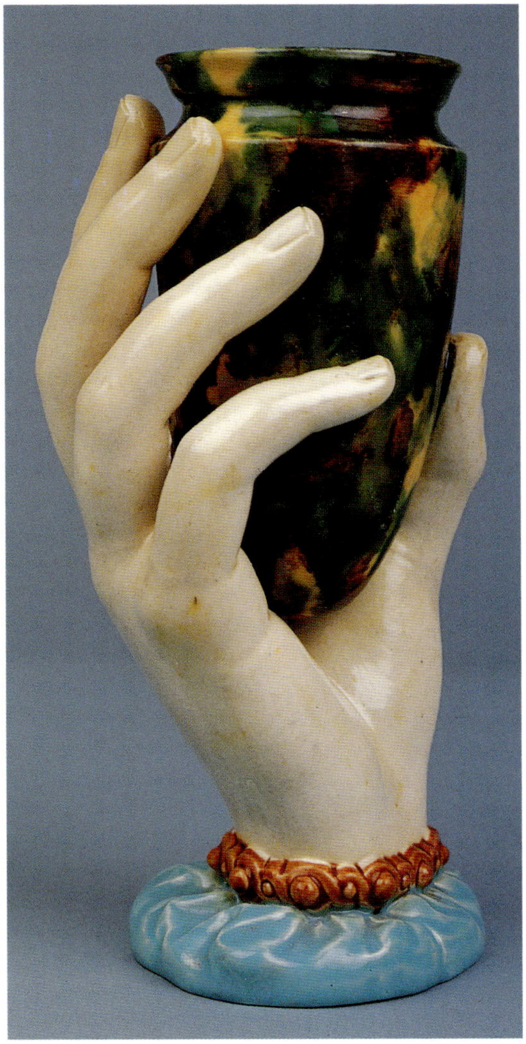

Hand holding tortoiseshell glazed flower vase, Royal Worcester, 6" h. $700+.

Cobalt ground vase with butterfly, puttis, flowers, and insects in relief, Gerbing and Stefan (Bodenboch, Bohemia, producing high quality majolica from c. 1885-1910), 10" h. $400-440.

Back row, left to right: French figural ewer with oranges and twig handle, Menton; French figural lemon vase, Menton, 12"; French figural lemon vase with twig handles, Menton, 6.75". $500-800 each.
Front row, left to right: French lemon and floral vase, Menton, 6"; French miniature lemon ewer and orange ewer, Menton; Two part lemon figural salt, attributed to Massier, 4". $150-300 each.

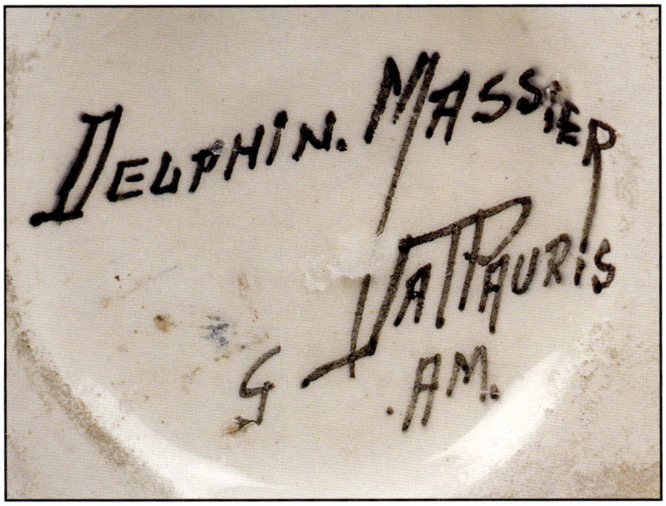

Stork vase, Delphin Massier, 8.5" h. $600-660.

Small flower-shaped vase, Delphin Massier, 5" h. $300-330.

Calla lily vase, Jerome Massier, 6" h. $600-660.

Bird and fruit figural vase, Fives-Lille (De Bruyn factory, Lille, France, 1862-1962; production of barbotine [French term applied to majolica and faience wares with high relief, thin decorations including flowers] begins in 1887 and majolica is listed in company catalogs from 1905-1938; the company manufacturer's mark consists of an anchor with the initials D and B applied over it.), 12" h. $500-550.

Pair of French figural lemon vases, artist-signed "L. Berty", 13.5" h. In 2004, these signed vases brought $700 at auction.

French figural ostrich vase, unmarked, 8.25" h. $200-300.

A pair of Continental Moorish figural floral vases, unmarked, 11.75" h. $400-600 each.

Pair of Blackamoor figural vases with a man and woman holding baskets, unmarked, 12" h. $600-800 each.

Wall pockets

Maiden wall pocket, Minton. This beautiful wall pocket sold at auction in 2004 for $2,100.

A rare bird's nest and bird wall pocket with fitted wooden back plate, Wedgwood, 12" w., 9" h. $850-935.

Rose wall pocket, Delphin Massier, 9" h. $700-770.

French dog in basket wall pocket, unmarked, 13" h. $600-660.

Entryway

Victorian etiquette required gentlemen and ladies to leave their umbrellas and walking sticks in umbrella stands in the entryway upon entering the Victorian home. Large majolica umbrella stands were sure to make an impression on all who entered or exited through the front door.

Umbrella stands

Hunting theme majolica umbrella stand by S. Fielding & Co. The tree trunk base is decorated with a "bagged" rabbit and a mallard duck hanging off of the tree trunk. Fox glove flowers and leaves decorate the side of the tree stump. This umbrella stand measures 25" high and sold at auction in 2004 for $7,425.

Turquoise umbrella stand, S. Fielding & Co., 22.5" h. $800-1,000+.

Argenta "Crusader" three lobed umbrella/stick stand, Wedgwood. $1,000-1,500.

Last Words – Majolica's Significance

Opposite page:
For the Victorians, to prove you were up-and-coming you needed many beautiful objects. Majolica wares were among those items Victorians turned to when proving their worth. Turquoise nautilus shell supported by two mermen, shell has puttis in high relief and a maiden atop shell, Minton, shape no. 992, date code for 1874, 20.5" h, 17.5" w.

To truly understand majolica, one needs to understand how majolica wares were used and what they meant to the people who first purchased them. Driven by the engines of the Industrial Revolution, the Victorian age was a time of great social change. Families migrated from rural to urban environments, from an agrarian to a technological society. Job opportunities and increased income flowed to a growing middle class, with men and women entering the labor pool together. Consumer buying power was on the rise. These forces created an ambitious middle class striving to climb both the social and economic ladders of success. Social functions, such as dinners, became formal and intricate affairs designed to impress those who could help you rise to new heights. And for the Victorians, to prove you were up-and-coming you needed many beautiful objects. Majolica wares were among those items Victorians turned to when proving their worth.

In 1878, the *Pottery and Glass Trades' Review* reported that large orders for majolica were being placed by Americans for "the more expensive class of goods." (Bergensen 1989, 12) These were large majolica items such as the floor urn, centerpieces, and impressive figures displayed in the previous chapter. The article stated that majolica wares could be considered the most popular class of decorated pottery in 1878 for the American market and that demand was on the rise. Novel items were considered to be quick selling products.

In their decorative role, ornamental majolica wares displayed in homes stated that the families residing there were "genteel," people of refinement and good taste. This was of great significance to members of the Victorian middle class successful enough to strive to move into higher economic and social circles. It was also significant to those of lesser means and recent immigrants. These people tended to be looked down upon by society at large. To counter perceptions that they were coarse and vulgar folk, individuals in these groups would purchase a few ornate objects (many of the majolica decorative items would have been priced low enough to be within their reach), proclaiming to all who observed them that gentility resided in this humble home as well. Neighbors visited each other far more frequently then than they do today. Among those who were not upwardly mobile, the presence of ornamental ceramics was a source of pride and dignity they shared during visits, bolstering them against the misperceptions of others they faced when away from the security of home and friends.

This Victorian desire to project an air of cultural refinement was not limited to Americans. In 1893, an author for *The Potteries—Illustrated* reported on the situation in England's famous Staffordshire potting district. He observed that even in humble workers' homes groupings of statuary could be seen in windows, colorful decorative tiles were noted in patterns in doorways and on walls. When owners did not have the financial resources to purchase a set of tiles, a single tile prominently displayed added a grace note to the home.

Different cultures ascribed different meanings to ornamental ceramics as well. While in Victorian American culture at large, such items were statements of refinement and declarations of success in business, to the Irish, a cupboard full of ornamental objects spoke of other things. The Irish displayed the ceramics presented to them on important occasions, such as weddings, and those given to them by old friends and loved ones. To the Irish observer, that cabinet spoke of love and family history. No doubt those objects also launched many stories on quiet evenings when the day's work was done.

In fact, well made ornamental majolica objects would have been proudly presented as gifts on birthdays, weddings, and other significant occasions. Such impressive items would have spoken well of the love the gift giver felt for the recipient and would have reflected equally well upon the taste of the giver.

Well made ornamental majolica objects would have been proudly presented as gifts on birthdays, weddings, and other significant occasions. Such impressive items would have spoken well of the love the gift giver felt for the recipient and would have reflected equally well on the taste of the giver. This imposing Minton turquoise nautilus shell supported by two mermen impressed present-day collectors as well, bringing $10,000 at auction in 2004.

Bibliography

Albertson, Karla Klein. "The colorful creatures of majolica art." *Philadelphia Inquirer*, Friday, January 16, 2004.

Barber, Edwin Atlee. "Etruscan Majolica." *Bulletin of the Pennsylvania Museum*, Memorial Hall, Fairmount Park, Philadelphia, July 1907.

_____. *Marks of American Potters*. Philadelphia, Pennsylvania: Patterson & White Co., 1904.

Barbolla-Roland, Diane. "Maiolica at the San Diego Presidio Gateway Search Excavation: A Preliminary Analysis." *The Journal of San Diego History* 29(3), Summer 1983.

Bergensen, Victoria. *Majolica. British, Continental & American Wares 1851-1915.* London: Barrie & Jenkins, 1989.

Bockol, Leslie. *Victorian Majolica.* Atglen, Pennsylvania: Schiffer Publishing, 1996.

"A Brief History of the Pottery Industry." *Information Sheets.* Gladstone Pottery Museum. <http://www2002.stoke.gov.uk/museums/Gladstone/gpminf04.html>

Bunt, Cyril G. *British Potters and Pottery Today.* E. F. Lewis Publishers, Ltd., 1956.

"Burslem." *The Potteries—Illustrated Directory*, n.d.

Carter, Susan N. "Ceramic Art at the Exhibition." *Appleton's journal: a monthly miscellany of popular literature* I(1), July 1876, pp. 74-77.

"Centennial Exhibition." *The Manufacturer and Builder*, November 1876, pp. 244-245.

Clement, Arthur W. *Our Pioneer Potters*. York, Pennsylvania: The Maple Press Company, 1948.

Cluett, Robert. *George Jones Ceramics 1861-1951.* Atglen, Pennsylvania: Schiffer Publishing, 1998.

_____. *Staffordshire Pottery: 1852-1962. Majolica, Transfer Prints, Flow Blue, Fine Bone China from Cauldon.* Atglen, Pennsylvania: Schiffer Publishing, 2004.

Cunningham, Helen. *Majolica Figures.* Atglen, Pennsylvania: Schiffer Publishing, 1997.

Cushion, John P. and William B. Honey. *Handbook of Pottery & Porcelain Marks.* 4th ed. London: Faber & Faber, 1980.

Dawes, Nicholas M. *Majolica.* New York: Crown Publishers, Inc., 1990.

Dessoie, Mary. "Looking for a small, elegant collectible? Here's the pat answer." *The Old Times* 14(6), March 2001.

DuBay, Debby. *Antique Limoges at Home.* Atglen, Pennsylvania: Schiffer Publishing, 2002.

Elliott, Charles Wyllys. "Pottery at the Centennial." *The Atlantic Monthly* 38(229), November 1876, pp. 568-597.

"Famous Potters of Stoke-on-Trent. Thomas Minton 1765-1836." <http://net1.netcentral.co.uk/steveb/potters/minton.html>

Freyer, Bryna. "101 Ways Not To Eat With Your Fingers: The Great Era of American Silverplate." Presented to the Culinary Historians of Washington, D.C., December 2, 2001. <http://www.chowdc.org/Papers/Feyer%202001.html>

Fryatt, F. E. "Pottery in the United States." *Harper's New Monthly Magazine* 62(369), February 1881, pp. 357-370.

"Glazing of Pottery Without Lead." *Manufacturer and Builder* 7(5), May 1875.

Godden, Geoffrey A. *Encyclopedia of British Pottery and Porcelain Marks.* New York: Bonanza Books, 1964.

Hume, Ivor Noël. *All the Best Rubbish*. New York: Harper & Row, Publishers, 1974.

"Increase of English Industries Since Exhibition of 1851." Unattributed article.

Johnson, Don. "Majolica Auction." *Maine Antique Digest*, June 2000.

_____. "Majolica Auction." *Maine Antique Digest*, July 2001.

Karmason, Marilyn G. "Majolica On Both Sides of the Atlantic." *Antique Trader*, March 29, 2000.

Karmason, Marilyn G. and Joan B. Stacke. *Majolica. A Complete History and Illustrated Survey.* New York: Harry N. Abrams, 1989.

Katz-Marks, Mariann. *The Collector's Encyclopedia of Majolica: An Identification and Value Guide.* Paducah, Kentucky: Collector Books, 1992.

Knowles, Eric. "Minton's masterpieces." <http://www.essentialhomes.com>.

Kowalsky, Arnold A. and Dorothy E. *Encyclopedia of Marks on American, English, and European Earthenware, Ironstone, and Stoneware.* Atglen, Pennsylvania: Schiffer Publishing, 1999.

Liebeknecht, William B. "Joseph Mayer's Arsenal Pottery Dump. Part 2: Majolica." *Trenton Potteries: Newsletter of the Potteries of Trenton Society* 1(3), August/September 2000 .

"Majolica." *Manufacturer and Builder* 8(11), November 1876, p. 257.

McCutcheon, Marc. *The Writer's Guide to Everyday Life in the 1800s*. Cincinnati, Ohio: Writer's Digest Books, 1993.

Moore, N. Hudson. *The Old China Book*. New York: Tudor Publishing Company, 1903.

Murray, D. Michael. *European Majolica.* Atglen, Pennsylvania: Schiffer Publishing, 1997.

Peterson, Harold L. *Americans At Home*. New York: Charles Scribner's Sons, 1971.

Pool, Daniel. *What Jane Austen Ate and Charles Dickens Knew*. New York: Simon & Schuster, 1993.

"The Potteries and Their Environs. A descriptive account of The Potteries (illustrated) 1893 advertising and trade journal." *The Potteries—Illustrated*, Trade Directory Index, 1893.

"Pottery & Porcelain – American." Notebook, 1993. <http://www.noteaccess.com/APPROACHES/DecorativeAA/Pamerican2.html>

"Preservation." *Centre County Architecture.* <http://centrecountyhistory.org/ccarch3.html>

"Preservation." *Centre County Architecture.* <http://centrecountyhistory.org/ccarch4.html>

"Progress of the Pottery Industries." *Manufacturer and Builder* 12(4), April 1880.

Punchard, Lorraine. *Playtime Pottery & Porcelain: From the United Kingdom & the United States*. Atglen, Pennsylvania: Schiffer Publishing, 1996.

Rickard, Jonathan. "Major Magical Majolica Surprise." *Maine Antique Digest*, August 1998.

Schneider, Mike. *Majolica.* Atglen, Pennsylvania: Schiffer Publishing, 1990.

Sheehan, Virginia. " 'Young clean catholic general maid seeking a situation': Evidence of Domestic Service in the Ottawa Archaeological Record." A Collection of Papers Presented at the 33rd Annual Meeting of the Canadian Archaeological Association. The Ontario Archaeological Society, Inc. 2001.

Skinner, Tina (ed.). *Victorian Architecture.* Atglen, Pennsylvania: Schiffer Publishing, 2004.

Solis-Cohen, Lita. "The Harriman Judd Sale of British Art Pottery." *Maine Antique Digest*, April 2001.

Snyder, Jeffrey B. *Collecting Oyster Plates.* Atglen, Pennsylvania: Schiffer Publishing, 2002.

_____. *Marvelous Majolica.* Atglen, Pennsylvania: Schiffer Publishing, 2001.

_____. *Weller Pottery*. Atglen, Pennsylvania: Schiffer Publishing, 2005.

Snyder, Jeffrey B. and Leslie Bockol. *Majolica: British, American, & European Wares.* 2nd Edition. Atglen, Pennsylvania: Schiffer Publishing, 2001.

Spillman, Jane Shadel, Jorg Zutter, and J. Patrice Marandel. "Acquisitions." *The World of Antiques & Arts*. <http://www.antiquesandart.com.au/article.cfm?article=66>

"The Victorian Age." *Centre County Architecture* <http://centrecountyhistory.org>

"Victorian House" *Centre County Architecture* <http://centrecountyhistory.org>

Weidner, Brooke. *Catalog of Majolica 1884.* Phoenixville, Pennsylvania: Brooke Weidner, 1960 (reprint of the 1884 Griffen, Smith & Company World's Industrial and Cotton Centennial Exposition catalog).

Williams, Danielle. "Contemporary to Colonial. Powerhouse Museum." *Artwrite* Issue 20, 2002. <http://www.artwrite.cofa.unsw.edu.au/0020/2020 pages/Danielle_Williams.html>

Wilson, Susan. "An Elephant's Tale. An Unadulterated and Relatively True Story Chronicling the Life, Death, and Afterlife of Jumbo, Tufts' Illustrious Mascot." *Tufts online Magazine.* Spring 2002.

Wrenn, Sara B. "Oregon Folklore Studies." *Federal Writers' Project*. Washington, D.C.: Works Progress Administration, December 12, 1938.

Index

Albino, 42
Alcock & Co., Samuel, 137
Antiquarians, 10, 18
Appleton's Journal, 38
Arabia Pottery, 35
Argenta, 21, 42, 48, 157, 175, 176, 181, 182, 186, 202, 233
Arnoux, Jean François Léon, 9, 20, 30
Arsenal Pottery, 42-43
Art Nouveau, 18, 31, 35
Arts and Crafts Movement, 17, 18
Ashtrays, 22
Asparagus covered barrel, undertray, 133
Asparagus cradles, 132, 133, 134
Asparagus plates, 131, 132, 134, 135
Asparagus platters, 132
Asparagus sauce boats, 132
Asparagus sets, 32, 34, 130-135
Asparagus trays and cradles, 131
Asparagus-artichoke services, 32
Atlantic Monthly, 39
Australia, 7
Australian potters, 13

B. Bloch & Co., 33, 34, 35, 111, 112
Banks, 5, 105
Barbotine, 225
Barnum & Bailey Circus, 12
Barnum, Phineas T., 12
Barol, Jean, 30
Baskets, ornamental, 206
Bedrooms, 5, 56, 58, 59-63
Bennett, Edwin, 37, 39
Bennett, William, 39
Berry sets, 34
Berty, L., 226
Bevington, J. & T., 77
Billiard-/Smoking-room, 57, 58, 107-114
Bohemia, 33
Bookshelves, 206
Bottles, figural, 34, 77
Boudoir, 56, 58, 65
Boudoir/library/study, 58, 63-64
Bowls, 42, 43, 135-137
Boxes, 59, 60
Breakfast room/sitting room, 56, 58, 65-76
Brownfield & Son, William, 24, 27, 70, 78, 201, 208, 218, 219
Brownhills, 20
Brown-Westhead, Moore & Company, T.C., 24, 48
Bud vases, 115
Burslem, 20
Butter boats, 65
Butter dishes, 137-139
Butter pats, 42, 50, 74, 130, 140-142
Butter tubs, 139

Cachepots, 16, 115, 116-118
Cake plates, 65, 130
Cake stands, 142-143
Candle holders, candlesticks, 24, 34, 59, 61, 62
Carr, James, 37, 39
Carter, Susan N., 38
Centennial Exhibition, Philadelphia, Pennsylvania, 37, 38, 39
Centerpieces & center bowls, 8, 22, 34, 39, 130, 191-194
Chandeliers, 207
Chargers, 144
Cheese domes & keepers, 22, 48, 49, 145-151
Chesapeake Pottery Company, 42
Chestnut servers, 152
Choisy-le-Roi, 30, 42, 126
Cigar holders, 34
Cigars, 107
Clews, James, 39
Cobridge, 20
Coffee pots, 65, 71
Coffee services, 32
Comports, 20, 24, 39, 42, 130, 153-158
Condiment servers, 159
Conservatories, 5, 7, 57, 58, 54, 115
Conservatory/porch/garden, 58, 115-129
Console bowls, footed, 24
Continental potters, 20
Cooks, 77
Copeland & Sons, W.T., 24, 48, 121, 140, 220
Copeland & Sons Ltd., W.T., 7
Copyright, 45
Copyright Reserved, 46
Country of Origin, 46
Cradles, asparagus, 132, 133, 134
Creamers, 43, 65, 66, 67, 70, 71, 73
Creamers, child's, 106
Creamers, figural, 73
Creamers, strawberry, 190
Crown Princess of Prussia, 20
Crystal Palace Exhibition, 20, 37
Cup plates, 65
Cups and saucers, 25, 65, 73, 74, 75, 76
Cups and saucers, child's, 106

Darwin, Charles, 10, 15
De Medici, Catherine, 28
Decanter, 93
Della Robbia, Lucca, 9, 38
Designed or Made Expressly For, 46
Desk sets, 5
Dessert services, 32, 130
Dining room, 5, 57, 58, 130-205
Dishes, covered, 42
Dishes, game pie, 39, 48, 51, 160, 162
Dishes, sauce, 74, 188
Dishes, shrimp, 137
Downing, Andrew Jackson, 53
Drawing room, 6, 65
Drawing room/parlor, 57, 58, 206-230
Dressler, Julius, 33, 34

E. & W. Bennett, 39
Earthenware, soft-bodied, 7
Edward Steele, 71
Edwin Bennett Pottery, 39
Egg cups, 65
Egg holders, 65
Elliott, Charles Wyllys, 39
England, 46
Entryway, 5, 57, 58, 231-232
Etruria, 20
Etruscan, 40, 42, 45
Etruscans, 10
Eureka Pottery, 42, 101, 102
Ewer and basin sets, 24, 59
Ewers, 26-27, 34, 223
Ewers, ornamental, 208
Exhibitions, 28
Exhibitions, Centennial, 1876, 37, 38, 39
Exhibitions, Crystal Palace, 9, 37
Exhibitions, Paris, 1867, 1878, 1889, 30, 36

Fabry, Joseph, 30
Faience, 225
Faience Manufacturing Company, 42
Federal Writers' Project, 104
Fejee mermaid, 12
Fenton, 20
Figural, 5, 6, 19, 48, 50, 54, 114, 234, 236, 209-212
Figurals, anthropomorphic & cheery, 106
First World War, 31
Five o'clock tea, 65
Fives-Lille, 225
Floor urns, 213
Flower holders, 115, 118
Flowerpots, 24, 54, 115
Flowers, morally uplifting, 115
Forester, Thomas, 24, 25, 120, 145
Fountain pen wipe, 63
Franco-Prussian War, 30
Fryatt, F.E., 43

Game dishes, game tureens, 160-162
Game pie dishes, 48, 51, 160-162
Garden seats, 39, 48, 115, 119-120
Gardens, 58, 115
George Jones & Sons, 10, 13, 16, 22, 23, 24, 44, 48, 49, 50, 51, 52, 62, 66, 73, 76, 80, 81, 82, 118, 119, 121, 122, 146, 147, 153, 154, 160, 163, 168, 169, 170, 171, 188, 189, 190, 191, 192, 195, 196, 207
Gerbing & Stefan, 222
Glaze colors, lead, 7
Gothic Revival, 53
Great Atlantic and Pacific Tea Company (A & P), 41
Griffen, George, 39
Griffen, Henry, 39, 42
Griffen, Love & Co., 42
Griffen, Smith & Co., 24, 37, 39, 40, 41, 42, 45, 70, 71, 74, 87, 88, 105, 136, 141, 176, 177, 178, 184, 200, 206
Griffen, Smith & Hill, 39, 40, 45
Group Sarreguemines, 30

Hair-tidy, 63
Hampshire Pottery, 42
Hanley, 20
Harper's New Monthly Magazine, 43
Heth, Joice, 12
Hill, William, 39, 45
Historicism, 18
Holdcroft, Joseph, 5, 24, 25, 48, 59, 60, 67, 73, 83, 84, 119, 123, 124, 135, 155, 171, 172, 186, 190
Hothouses, 115
House styles, 53-54
Housemaids, 77
Hugo Lonitz, 35, 54, 127, 194, 208, 211
Humidors, 34, 107-110

Industrial Revolution, 17, 115, 235
Inkwells, 11, 63-64
Italianate style, 53

J. & T. Bevington, 63, 77
J. Roth, 70
Jackson, Alexander, 53
Jacobi, Nicolas-Henri, 30
Jacobi, Paul-Augustin, 30
Japanese motifs, 16, 21, 30, 42
Jardinières, 32, 42, 43, 54
Jardinières, floor, 7, 121
Jardinières, footed, 122, 123
Jardinières, pedestaled, 5, 24, 34, 115
Jardinières, window, 124
Jardinières, with & without pedestals, 121-126
Jeffords, J. E., 37, 39
Job opportunities, 235
José A. Cunha, 36
Jugs, 32, 38, 42, 43
Jugs, face, 90-93
Jugs, Palissy ware, 96
Jugs, Toby, 77, 89, 97
Jugs, Tower, 85
Jumbo the elephant, 12

Karmason, Marilyn, 52
Keller & Guerin, 32, 133
Keller, Guerin & St. Clément, 32
Kitchen, 5, 58, 77-104

La Faïencerie d'Onnaing, 30, 31, 89
Ladle, strawberry, 190
Lamps, 34
Lane Delph, 20
Lane End, 20
Laurier House, 77
Lear, Samuel, 16
Lhermine, Emile, 32
Library, 5, 58
Library/study, 56
Limited, 45
Lincoln, Abraham, 38
Longchamp, 131, 132, 214
Longport, 20
Longton, 20
Lonitz, Hugo, 35, 54, 127, 194, 208, 211
Love, J. Stuart, 42

Made In, 46
Mafra and Sons, 36
Maid-of-all-work, 77
Maiolica, 9
Majolica, Australian, 13
Majolica, definition, 7
Majolica, located by room, 58
Majolica, significance, 234-235
Majorca, 9
Mansard or Second Empire style, 53
Mantle, 5, 206
Manufacture Royale de Rato, 36
Manufacturer and Builder, 9, 38
Manufacturer's Marks, 43-46
Manufacturers, majolica, 19-42
Manufacturers, majolica, in Britain, 20-27
Manufacturers, majolica, in the United States, 37-42
Manufacturers, majolica, on the Continent, 28-36
Marmalade pots, 65
Massier, 126
Massier, Clément, 30, 71
Massier, Delphin, 30, 31, 127, 167, 223, 224, 230
Massier, Jérôme, 30, 106, 128, 224
Massier-type, 115
Match boxes, strikers, & holders, 24, 34, 35, 39, 111-114
Match stands, 59
Mayer, James, 42
Mayer, Joseph, 42
Menton, 223
Milk pots, 65
Minton & Company, 8, 10, 11, 14, 19, 20, 22, 30, 38, 42, 48, 50, 51, 61, 68, 85, 111, 115, 116, 124, 125, 130, 144, 152, 159, 164, 165, 179, 190, 193, 197, 205, 209, 210, 215, 221, 229, 235, 236
Minton, Herbert, 9, 20, 37
Mintons, 44
Model of a Bull, 210
Moehling, 106, 111
Monogram, GSH, 39, 40, 45
Morley & Company, 42
Morris, William, 17
Mottahedeh & Co., Inc., 52
Moulin des Loups & Hamages, 32
Mugs, 66

Naturalism, 10
New Milford Pottery Company, 42
New York City Pottery, 39
Nimy-les-Mons, 89
Nursemaids, 77
Nursery/children's bedrooms, 56, 58, 105-106

Odell & Booth Brothers, 42
On the Origin of Species by Means of Natural Selection, 10, 15
Onnaing Society, 31
Orchies, 32, 89
Oyster plates, 5, 16, 22, 32, 163-167
Oysters, 130

Palissy, Bernard, 28, 38, 179
Palissy style, 28, 32, 36
Palissy ware, 39, 213
Paris Exhibition, 1867, 16
Paris Exposition, 1878, 39
Parlor, 5, 58
Parlormaids, 77
Patent Applied For, 46
Patented, 46
Peekskill Pottery Company, 42
Philadelphia City Pottery, 39
Pitchers, 5, 21, 23, 24, 31, 32, 33, 34, 39, 42, 43, 70, 77-104
Pitchers, cream, 42
Pitchers, figural, 31, 32, 33, 77, 84, 89-97
Pitchers, syrup, 65, 105
Place card holders, 22, 167
Planters, 28, 31, 54, 115, 127-128
Planters, hanging, 129
Plaques, 36
Plaques & trays, ornamental, 213-214
Plaques, wall, 34
Plates, 24, 34, 40, 42, 43, 65, 168-178, 182
Plates, asparagus, 131, 132, 134, 135
Plates, butter, 65
Plates, child's, 106
Plates, dessert, 130
Plates, dessert, 35, 168, 169, 170, 171
Plates, preserves, 65
Plates, strawberry, 190
Platters, 5, 9, 22, 40, 41, 42, 179-183
Platters, asparagus, 132
Platters, egg, 34
Podmore, Walker & Company, 21
Popularity, height of majolica's, 7
Porches, 53-54, 58
Potholes, 20
Potteries, The, 20
Potters, American, 37
Potters, Australian, 13
Potters, Continental, 20
Potters, European, 28
Pottery and Glass Trades' Review, 235
Pottery Gazette, 24
Preserve plates, 65
Preserve pots, 11
Punch bowls, Mr. Punch, 23
Punch bowls, sets, 184

Queen Anne style, 53
Queen Victoria, 12

Rafael Bordalo Pinheiro, 36
Registration Marks, 43, 44, 45, 46-47
Registration Numbers, 46
Renaissance, 9, 30
Reproductions, 51, 52
Ridgway, John, 39
Ring stands, 59
Romanticism, 10
Rörstrand Pottery, 35
Roth, J., 70
Row homes, 53
Royal Worcester, 69, 221
Royal, 45
Ruskin, John, 17

St. Clément, 32, 33, 93, 94
Salons, 57
Salts, individual, double, 130, 184-185
Samuel Alcock & Co., 137
Samuel Lear, 16
Sardine boxes, 22, 34, 39, 52, 186-187
Sardine dishes, 24
Sarreguemines, 28, 29, 30, 90, 91, 92, 129, 139, 203
Sarreguemines-type, 93
Sauce boats, asparagus, 132
Sauce dishes, 188
Saucers, 177
Schiller & Gerbing, 33, 34
Schneider, Georg, 35
Scott, Matthew "Scotty", 12
Seats, garden, 39, 115, 119-120
Sergent, Thomas-Victor, 126, 158, 185, 215
Servants, 77
Servers, 188
Servers, asparagus, 130
Servers, caviar, 22
Servers, chestnut, 152
Servers, condiment, 159
Servers, double shell, 25
Servers, oyster, 130
Servers, strawberries, 130, 189-190
Servers, strawberry, double, 10
Shelton, 20
Shelves, 215
Shorter & Son, 86
Shotgun houses, 53, 56
Sicard, Jacques, 30
Simon Fielding & Co., 24, 25, 76, 79, 140, 180, 231, 232
Sitting room, 5
Smith, David, 39, 42
Smoker's companions, 34
Smoking sets, 107, 112, 114
Social changes, 235
Société Anonyme, 32
South Kensington Exhibition, 1862, 16
Souvenirs, 38
Spill vases, 5, 58, 106, 215-216
Spittoons, 22, 24, 43
Spoon holders, Spooners, 42, 65
Spoons, strawberry, 190
Stafford Knot, 45
Staffordshire of America, Trenton, New Jersey, 43
Staffordshire potting district, England, 20
Steele, Edward, 71
Steins, 34
Stevens, Alfred, 20
Stoke-Upon-Trent, 20
Strawberry sets, 24
Study, 58
Sugar bowls, 65, 66, 70, 71
Sugar bowls, child's, 106

T.C. Brown-Westhead, Moore & Company, 24, 48
Table lamps, 217
Table services, 32
Tea gowns, 65
Tea sets, 5, 32, 42, 58, 66-76
Tea sets, children's or miniature, 5, 106
Tea tiles, 76
Teacups, 65
Teapots, 24, 42, 43, 65, 66, 67, 69, 70, 71, 72
Teapots, child's, 106
Teapots, figural, 15, 48, 68, 70
The Potteries—Illustrated, 235
Thomas Forester & Sons, Ltd., 24, 25
Thomas-Victor Sergent, 126, 158, 185, 215
Tiles, 36
Tobacco jars, 42
Toby jugs, 77
Toothpick holders, 195
Townhouses, 55
Toy services, 24
Trade Mark, 45
Trays, 13, 14, 37, 50, 51, 59, 65, 195-200
Trays and cradles, asparagus, 131
Trays, card, 34
Trays, comb, 59
Trays, serving, 14
Trays, trinket, 59
Tunstall, 20
Tureens, 24, 201-203
Tureens, game, 48, 161, 162

Umbrella stands, 5, 231-233
Underplate, sunflower, 105
United States Patent, 46
Universal Exhibition, Paris, 20
Urns, floor, 213
Urns, hot-water, 65
Utzschneider, François-Paul, 30

Values, majolica, 47-49
Vases, 18, 24, 25, 29, 32, 34, 39, 42, 218-228
Vases, basket, 24
Vases, Etruscan, 10
Vases, mantle, 220
Victoria Pottery Co., 69, 160, 161, 201
Villeroy & Boch, 34

Wall pockets, 34, 229-230
Wannopee Pottery Company, 42
Wardle & Co., 69, 70, 74, 111, 138
Wardle Art Pottery Co. Ltd., 69
Warranted, 46
Washington, George, 12, 38
Waste bowls, 65, 76
Wedgwood, 6, 9, 10, 14, 20, 21, 38, 39, 42, 44, 48, 74, 86, 118, 142, 156, 157, 162, 166, 167, 172, 173, 174, 175, 176, 180, 181, 182, 184, 186, 188, 193, 198, 199, 200, 202, 206, 230, 233
Wedgwood, Enoch, 21
Wedgwood, Josiah, 10, 21
Wedgwood, Josiah, & Sons Ltd., 6
Wedgwood, Ralph, 21
Wedgwoods, The Other, 21
Weightman, Margaret, 104
Weller Pottery, 30
Whatnot case, 206
Wilhelm Schiller & Sons, 33, 34, 195
Willets Manufacturing Company, 42
William Brownfield & Son, 24, 27, 70, 78, 201, 208, 218, 219
William Smith & Company, 21
William Tomlinson & Company, 21
Wine coolers, 204-205
Wood, Edmund T., 21
Wood, John Wedg, 21
Worcester Royal Porcelain Company, 69
Workrooms, 56
World's fairs, 9, 16, 20, 28, 39
World's Industrial and Cotton Centennial Exposition, 1884, 39